Research in Social Work

RESEARCH IN SOCIAL WORK

A.K. Patel
M.V. Dubey

CRESCENT
PUBLISHING CORPORATION

[*The responsibility for the facts stated, conclusions reached and plagiarism, if any, in this book is entirely that of the Author. And the Publisher bears no responsibility for them, whatsoever.*]

Research in Social Work

First Published : 2010

ISBN 978-81-8342-170-6

Published by :

CRESCENT PUBLISHING CORPORATION
4831/24, Prahlad Street,
Ansari Road, Darya Ganj,
New Delhi - 110002
Ph. : 23272541, 23257835
Fax : 91- 011- 23257835
e-mail : campusbooks@hotmail.com
commonwealth_pub@yahoo.com

Laser Typesetting by :
Anupama Computers
Delhi

Printed at :
Roshan Offset Printers
Delhi

Preface

Social work research addresses psychosocial problems, preventive interventions, treatment of acute and chronic conditions, and community, organisational, policy and administrative issues. Covering the lifespan, social work research may address clinical, services and policy issues. It benefits consumers, practitioners, policy-makers, educators, and the general public by examining prevention and intervention strategies for health and mental health, child welfare, aging, substance abuse, community development, managed care, housing, economic selfsufficiency, family well-being, etc. This book is intended to help inform policy, practice and education by providing information on social work research to student, as well as to the general public.

Research methods for social work have undergone several changes in the recent past, particularly in the areas of research designs, techniques of data collection, analysis of data and computer application in social work research. The book will give readers an insight into the various research methods used in different areas of social work and need for shift in focus. It will be a useful guide for social work practitioners to enhance the evidence base of their practice and would also serve as a resource for social work research students.

A.K. Patel
M.V. Dubey

Contents

1

Introduction to Social Work Research

The research process will be illustrated with five examples, four using hypothetical data and one using real data. These examples will include the entire research process from start to finish. Between them, these five examples will give you practical examples of most of the skills included in this chapter. Of course, five projects need five researchers, and here they are:

- Abigail is a PhD student who is interested in completing a project for an advanced research methods course. If all goes well, she plans to present it at a local conference.
- John is a new PhD student who is interested in the local Bosnian refugee community, with whom he has a little experience working. He is short of money and desperately wants to get a grant to help subsidise his education. He is hoping to do some qualitative pilot research to help him write a stronger multimethod (meaning both qualitative and quantitative) grant.
- Professor Kathy is a criminologist. Her work requires that her research assistants read through large numbers of handwritten and electronic police files to determine how many times each person in

the files has been arrested and convicted, and of what offenses. Each of her research assistant coders fills out a summary form on each person's file. The problem is that her research assistants are accurate only about 80% of the time. She knows this because she has had other people check their work. Professor Kathy is desperate to do just about whatever she can to reduce errors. One afternoon, she heard a radio programme on National Public Radio (all professors listen to NPR, it is written into our contracts) talking about an organisation that uses classical music, which they claimed decreased clerical errors. Professor Kathy decided she would try this to see how well it might work. The more she thought about it, the more she thought it might be a good thing to really try it out scientifically. Maybe she could get a publication out of it too.

– Maria is a master's level student specialising in research. She is interested in homicide rates. What kinds of people kill each other? Where do all these killings occur? She is hoping to use this question for her master's research specialisation project, and she thinks it would be fun to do something at a conference, maybe to present a poster.
– Yuan is a master's student who has a field placement at a domestic violence facility that treats batterers. The agency is thinking of changing the treatment model they use and has asked Yuan to help them figure out if the new model will work better than the old model. Yuan is taking this opportunity to use the research for his treatment evaluation course project.

Area of Interest

The good news is that you probably have an area of

interest. For most people, there is an area that they want to understand better. Often it has to do with prior personal or professional experience. Sometimes it is something you enjoy thinking about. The challenge is taking a broad area of interest and turning it into something that can generate useful research questions. Areas of interest can be narrow or broad. One senior professor at our school is fond of telling students that "not all questions are created equal." We agree. A good area of interest will meet the following requirements:

— *Your area should interest you.* People often choose to study something because it is easy to study or because there are other people around them studying it, or because their school has very strong resources in that area. This is generally a mistake. Most people can do their best work only if they are care about the thing being studied. Choose something that does not interest you, and you may find yourself "running out of gas," getting easily irritated, and being unhappy. These are bad things that can be avoided by finding a way to do what you want to do.

— *You must be able to say what your area of interest is in one sentence in simple language.* The mother of one of the authors used to say, "If you can't say it simply then you don't understand it." If you can't spit it out in simple English, then you need to think some more.

— *Your area of interest must be small enough to guide you to specific questions.* "Children," "Behaviour," and "Diversity" are so broad as to be not very helpful. Areas that are more focused, such as "Barriers to academic performance in young children," or "Differences in altruistic behaviour between men and women," or "Child-rearing practices among the

Hmong in America" are more targeted and will allow you to move more easily to specific questions.

— *Your area should have some relevance to practice.* Unless you are doing purely basic science, your area of interest will need to be one that can inform what is going on in the field. As you recall, basic science means "science that is meant to find out about things but has no goal of immediate practical application." This is different from applied science, which is science that is intended to have an impact on the real world right now. Physics is a basic science, while engineering is the corresponding applied science. In the social sciences, sociology is commonly basic science, psychology has large basic and applied branches, while social work and counselling are usually applied.

— *Your area should be important. We* suppose that all events are important to the people they happen to, but some things are far more important or are more in need of research than others. Does your area really matter? What practical benefits to humankind would come about if we knew more about your area? Issues that affect many other areas of life, such as increasing literacy or decreasing poverty, are clearly very important. This is both a practical issue and one that concerns values and ethics. Is it reasonable to waste resources on something irrelevant? Are you making the world a better place? Is there a reasonable chance that some real moral good will come from the proposed work?

— *Your area must lead to questions you can study both ethically and practically.* This means that in your area you must be able to:

1. *Specify measurable variables:* For example, "unease" is not a commonly measured

construct, but there are scads of ways to study "depression." Even depression might be hard to measure for some people, for example people with serious illnesses for which standardised scales cannot be used.

2. *Collect the information for the variables ethically:* For example, let's say an individual is interested in stress levels among hostages during bank robberies. Because of the stress, retrospective recall is particularly bad among hostages, so asking them afterward has limitations. The simplest thing would be to stage a robbery yourself and observe people as it went down. Of course, this would almost certainly hurt people and is totally unethical. Likewise, it would be extremely dangerous if the researcher tried to use "participant observation" and pose as a criminal to be included in a planned robbery. It would also be unethical not to warn the authorities to try to prevent the crime. In short, you will have very limited ways that you can ethically study stress among hostages, and you will need to think creatively. Maybe you can use voice-stress analyses?

3. *Justify access to the study population:* If you are going to interact with human subjects, then the question should be important enough to justify the intrusion-even if the questions to be asked are "harmless" and not time consuming. Part of this includes consideration of the perspective of the group to be studied. For example, part of being culturally competent is understanding if the group to be studied also values this particular line of research. Further, if possible, you want to avoid sampling from a vulnerable

population. For example, minors, prisoners, and individuals with developmental or mental health disabilities are considered "vulnerable populations." These individuals are considered to have limited abilities to consent to participate in research for various reasons. You must have a very important reason to include such individuals in your sample. There must be a clear benefit to the subject group (either immediately or in the future) that far outweighs consideration of their vulnerability. Even with such a rationale, human subjects clearance will be difficult, and you will have to do lots of extra work to show others (and to be sure yourself) that you aren't taking advantage of these vulnerable people.

4. *Obtain human subjects clearance from your institutional review board (IRB) and perhaps IRBs of participating agencies:* This is done by demonstrating that the study is important and can be conducted with consent and without harm to the subjects.

5. *Locate sufficient numbers of subjects:* Some subjects are just plain hard to find. For example, you might be interested in finding out what kinds of people are more likely to commit suicide. You decide to give people personality tests and then follow them to see if they end up killing themselves. Fortunately, very few people kill themselves, so you would have to start with literally thousands of people to end up with enough completed suicides to be meaningful.

6. *Execute the research with the resources available to you:* Do you have the money and time to do it? Do the tools you need exist?

- *Abigail,* who is interested in organisations and used to be a child welfare worker, has realised that "organisations" or "child welfare organisations" are probably too big an area to study. She thinks she might look at organisational climate as it affects workers. She is very uncertain as to what specific areas to look at. She thinks she might have a look at burnout, worker retention, and ways workers cope with stress. She might then see which area makes most sense to look at.
- *John* is a new PhD student who isn't sure what he wants to do. He is sure he wants to do work that can lead to a dissertation grant. Dissertation grants are nice because they provide both evidence to future employers of your skills and money to do research. John has always been interested in refugees and resettlement, because he thinks that the time that a person or family is in transition may be critical in getting them a good or a poor start in their new home. It seems like an important area. Locally, the largest population of recent immigrants consists of about 30,000 Bosnian refugees. John understands that this group of refugees has a high likelihood of having had traumatic experiences prior to coming to the United States and wonders how they are dealing with those experiences. John needs to find out more about refugees and their adjustment, and he also needs to go out to the community to see what's going on firsthand.
- *Professor Kathy* has a relatively easy time formulating a question: "Does background music change the number of mistakes made when coding files?" She is not sure yet what kind of music she will try out, or how many different types. She'll look at the literature first.

— *Maria* is interested in homicide rates. She needs to produce a "master's research specialisation project" by the end of the semester. She is interested in murder rates in different types of communities. Maria recently went to the dentist, where she noticed that the dentist had a computer screen that showed exactly where her fillings were. The more she thought about it, the more it amased her that even her cavities were in a database. If cavities exist in a database, then surely many other important things must exist, somewhere, electronically. Maria decided to track down a database that would tell her about murders and then try to see what she could find about the kinds of places in which murders occur. She fired up her search engine and was on her way.

— *Yuan* is having his question more or less thrust upon him. Yuan is interested in domestic violence and how it is treated. Because of this interest, he is working in a domestic violence shelter during his master's practicum (internship). As part of his education, Yuan is required to do research on the practicum site. For the past several months,Yuan's agency has been wondering if it should switch to a different model of treatment that features cognitive behavioural treatment (CBT) methods. Yuan suggests to the agency that they might want to try it out in a scientific way and see if it works better. The agency, pleased to have someone who brings some research interest and skill, has decided to have Yuan work on the evaluation process as part of his practicum. Yuan's question, therefore, is, "At our agency, will subjects treated by CBT do differently than clients treated under our old system?" Yuan is one lucky dude, having found both a question and a site.

Initial Literature Review

The process of learning more about your area of interest is usually called the literature review. We find this term misleading, because there are many resources available to you that are neither journal articles nor books nor book chapters. Among the other places you can go to find out more about your area are the Internet, conferences, professional organisations, colleagues, and experts in the area.

In fact, if you are at a university, your first step should probably be to have an informal chat with someone who already knows about the literature in your area, so that he or she can give you pointers as to how to proceed with your search. Don't be afraid to use the professors at your school. It is their job to help you learn. You will note that this section is titled "The Initial Literature Review." This is because you will keep finding more relevant sources throughout your work, and the purpose of this first section is to help you get enough stuff so that you can make some sense of the literature, not so that you are "finished." "Finishing" never happens in an absolute sense; there is always more to learn.

Types of Literature

Most sources can be described in the following ways:

- *Empirical:* These are mainly focused on presenting new data. Most articles and many book chapters are empirical. Example: An article reporting findings from an experimental treatment for autism, or a study describing relationships between neighbourhood poverty and rates of domestic violence.
- *Review or overview:* These sources tell you what we know about something. These are commonly found in book chapters and also in journals. Example: An

article describing what we know about what works and what fails in welfare-towork programmes.

- *Theoretical or conceptual:* These sources present ideas, tie together prior findings in new ways, or seek in some other manner to make sense out of what we know. Example: An article suggesting that the current findings in a given area can be best explained through the application of a new theoretical model.
- *Other:* Other articles can be found that focus on subjects such as research methodology or the application of research findings to specific policies.

The above terms are commonly used, but most sources are mixtures of these categories. For example, many empirical articles have literature review sections that are longer than their methods and results sections.

Where to find literature

There are many places where literature lurks. The main ones include the following:

- *Journal articles:* Journal articles are the lifeblood of science. If you pursue research as a career, you will consume more of these than anything else, and you will be judged on how often and how well you write them. There will be "core" journals in your area. For a child abuse researcher, examples might include Child Maltreatment, Child Abuse and Neglect, Child Welfare, and Children and Youth Services Review. However, such a researcher would also use many journals not in his or her core, such as Journal of Interpersonal Violence and Child Development.
- *Books and book chapters:* More books exist than you might think.
- *Governmental (or similar) publications:* Again, government publications are far more common than

you might expect and are often overlooked. Many are also free and can be ordered online from the government. Many are viewable online.

There are several basic approaches that we have found helpful in locating literature. You may develop others based on your area and personal style. We have listed them in the order we would pursue them in.

- *Ask the experts:* Go to a professor or other student in your area. Ask for quick suggestions regarding the key journals, texts, and government publications are in your area. Take no more than five minutes doing this. The idea is to get pointed in the right direction, not to have them do your work for you. Say something like "Hi. I'm so-and-so, and I'm interested in diabetes among Latinos. If you were me, what journals or books would you use to begin to understand that area better? Are there a few studies or a few researchers I should definitely look up?"
- *Online database searches:* At our university, we have access to Psychinfo, which is a good database with many journal articles and book titles listed. This is the best general resource for many people, although other excellent database search engines exist, such as Medline and Sociofile. Many universities have search programmes that allow you to search multiple databases at the same time.

Using search engines

Students come to us all the time saying, quite authoritatively, "There is no literature in my area." These students are always wrong. Why? Because they are just learning how to do searches and aren't really doing a very effective job yet. Using the following technique to isolate areas of interest and find overlaps will probably help you to do a better job.

- *The goal of searching-Finding areas of overlap:* You might want to know about cocaine-exposed infants. This requires you to find two issues simultaneously-cocaine exposure and infants. When you get only the articles that have both, you will have your stuff.
- *The technique of searching:* Effectively searching a database is a bit of an art and requires practice. The main skills you need to learn for advanced searching involve embedded "and" and "or" commands and learning where to put your parentheses. We will assume you are using a search engine like Psychinfo, which provides windows for entering search terms. Do this:

  1. *Think about how to specify each area in a very inclusive way,* for example, drug or substance or cocaine, and infant or prenatal or perinatal or newborn or child. You need not be perfect the first time; as you find articles, you will learn the key buzzwords and can redo your search, but you've got to start somewhere. In many engines, you have multiple windows to use. Each of these windows will function like a set of closed parentheses.
  2. *In the search window, type in a request for the intersection of these areas:* (drug or substance or cocaine) and (infant or prenatal or perinatal or newborn or child). If multiple windows are available, just type "drug" or "substance" or "cocaine" in the first window, check the "and" connector between the windows, and then type the rest of the text in the second window.
  3. *See how your search goes and revise 1 and 2 above.* For example, "drug" may give you too many false hits, and you may need to exclude it.

You can also search for articles by specific authors, using their names and specifying that you are looking for the author's name. In many search engines you can write this as "au=Smith." You can also specify years of publication, language, and type of subject. There is no substitute for just messing around with the search engines. You may well be frustrated for the first hour or two, but you will soon gain skill and speed in your searching. Most people find it kind of fun after they get used to it.

Hand review of core journals

After a bit of online searching, you will say to yourself something like, "Geez, the Journal of Imperialist Oppression is coming up everywhere!" Why not go right to the mother lode? Hit the library, get the last 5-10 years of JOIO, pile them up on an empty table, and look through every issue's table of contents. This takes less time than you think, and when you find an article it is already in your hands! Focus on recent journals. If you have online access to the journal in question, you can do this on your computer, and then download or print the articles you want.

Bibliography searches

Now you're getting hot. You've got lots of articles already. What is the next step? Look at the articles that are closest to what you are interested in. Read the bibliographies. Obviously, if you see good articles you don't have, you need to go get them, especially if they are cited over and over again in different articles. There are other clever things you can do too. Do some journals keep coming up time after time? If so, and you haven't already reviewed that journal, go do it. Do some author names keep coming up time after time? If so, go do an online search under that person's name.

Library catalogues

Your library probably has an electronic database with books and book chapters. Use it.

Library shelves

Hey, you've found the Library of Congress numbers for your subject, so get your bad self up to the stacks and look at all the books near the ones you found. Chances are you'll find more.

Surfing

Use a search engine and cruise the Net. Everyone knows how to do this already. Make sure you keep track of where you go and make sure that the sources you use are high-quality. DHHS is the Waiamea Bay of human services research Web surfing. Go there. You can find out about what's funded, and you can pull boatloads of documents. Once you find key people or institutions relevant to your work, go and track them down online. Many professors have their CVs or cool home pages online, which is a good way to get a listing of their work.

How to Physically Obtain Literature

There are two things you need to know:

(1) The best sources are always unavailable, and

(2) journal articles can sense desperation and are good at hiding.

For these reasons, you should look for sources at least a month in advance of needing them. We procrastinate as much as anyone else, but this is the one place where you will get roadkilled if you procrastinate too much. With these warnings in mind, you will want to find your sources in the following locations:

– *Off the shelves:* Most journals and books are allegedly on the shelves. Go grab the journals and photocopy them. At the start of a project you will seem to spend more time photocopying than sleeping. Do not check out books unless you want the whole book. Photocopy the pertinent chapter(s) instead.

- *Online copies (Internet):* Increasingly, full text versions of articles are available online. This is great. Download them to a special directory you create for that purpose. You may want to print them out on paper anyway, both for ease of use and security.
- *Through your Library System:* Your library may have special features that allow access to things that you can't get to online. Find out about what you have available. Your library almost certainly has an interlibrary loan system. This may be paper or electronic. In either case, you need to allow "several weeks for delivery" in our experience, even if your library claims to be able to deliver things much faster. Somehow that key reference always has something funny going on with it, and you have to wait.
- *Photocopying:* To repeat: Photocopy everything. We sometimes even photocopy chapters of books that we own (makes it possible to file them or put them in relevant binders). The first thing you must do is make absolutely sure that the date, publisher, journal title, book title, page numbers, author, book editor and whatever else you need for the citation is on the thing you are photocopying. If it isn't, write it in immediately. The first time you fail to do this and spend three hours trying to track something down, you will understand why.
- *Spending money:* There are some things you just plain need. Don't buy too little. Don't buy too much. Buy things that are otherwise unobtainable that you will refer to on a daily or weekly basis.

How to Physically Store Literature

Stuff gets away from you. This is bad. Prevent it in the following manner:

- *Create directories on your computer for pdf or similar downloaded articles.* In the last year or two it has finally become possible to do useful lit searches almost fully online. Increasingly large numbers of articles can be downloaded, commonly in.pdf format. If you can, do it! Make sure you keep these articles somewhere safe, preferably on a backed-up network drive or periodically copied to disks.
- *Use a computer reference manager such as Endnotes.* This allows you to quickly find stuff, and you can put bibliographies together automatically. The earlier you start doing this, the easier your life will be.
- *Keep a list of whom you loan what to. When* people want to borrow your material, give them a specific date you need it back. Keep a little notebook indicating whom you loaned what to. Write your name on everything you own in thick permanent felt marker on the outside. That way, even if they don't return it, they'll feel guilty each time they use it.

Examples of Preliminary Literature Searches

John's literature on bosnian refugees

John needs to find out about refugees in general, Bosnian refugees in particular, and what we know about what makes them adjust better to our society. Unfortunately, there is nobody else in his school studying this population. He goes to a professor during office hours who teaches a human diversity course who is able to point him to some basic theoretical articles on refugee resettlement.

One of these articles seems to provide a useful conceptual guide for how to think about the entire immigration experience. He then does a PsychInfo search using (Bosnian or Bosnia) and (immigrant or immigration or refugee), which provides 49 hits (a nice, reviewable number). This gets him a number of sources. In selecting which resources he would focus on, John favoured those articles that were empirical, that helped him understand the theory and the literature, and that were published in better journals.

John's next step was to obtain these articles physically and to obtain the key and commonly cited references in the sources, particularly from the dissertation and the review article. This provided him with a nice collection of about 40 articles. A number of trends in the literature are becoming apparent to John. First, there has been some fairly advanced empirical research, but almost exclusively in the area of PTSD, as John suspected. Second, almost all the empirical work has been done in the last few years, with few useful items being more than three years old. Third, there seems to be substantial current interest in this area, with publications in top journals.

This all seems to bode well for John's choice for a dissertation topic, since it is a hot issue which has apparently only been studied along the single axis of PTSD. John never did find a journal which seemed to come up repeatedly in the search, but he did find a sufficient literature base to support his further work. His challenge now is finding an interesting and understudied part in this area which will provide the best fit for his dissertation work.

Maria's literature on homicide rates

Maria, who is interested in community homicide rates, took a backward approach to exploring her area. She started by looking for data she could find online that measured homicide rates. She did a number of Web searches and found that while it was fairly easy to get data at the county level on homicides, it was tough finding anything at a lower level. While Maria had not initially thought about looking at suicide rates, the data were available, and it did seem interesting. Would it follow the same patterns as homicides? She found the question interesting and exciting.

Maria talked to the professor teaching her social development class about where she could get community data on zip codes to match to the San Diego data. She was told that the U.S. Census was the best source. A look at the census data dictionary showed her that she could easily find out a large number of interesting things about the residents of each zip code, including income, educational status, racial composition, median age, and so on. Maria now had a source for counts by zip code of suicide and homicide and a source for lots of other information about those zip codes that she could look at. She now had to find out what we know about community homicide and suicide rates.

Yuan's literature on domestic violence

Yuan first went to his agency to find what empirical literature they were aware of. He found several articles suggesting how treatment should be done but not much with evidence behind it. He then decided to look in the textbooks he had, but again, there were few empirical citations. He decided to do a Psychinfo search. Initially, he got few hits, but he eventually stumbled on the terms ("domestic violence," or batterer) and ("cognitive behavioural," or CBT).

Yuan has been fortunate, finding authoritative sources and three dissertations on the subject in the last 10 years. The dissertations should be particularly useful, because critiquing methodology as it exists in the field is often a primary focus of doctoral dissertations, and he should be able to build on their work and benefit from their experience.

Professor Kathy's literature on the effects of music

Professor Kathy did a search using (kw: music or kw:musical) and (kw: task or kw: performance or kw: completion). This resulted in 2,310 hits-too many. She narrowed her search to citations with these terms in the titles and switched "ti" for "kw," which dropped the results down to 379.

There seem to be several threads of research. First of all, there is research finding perhaps a slight benefit to music in terms of people doing repetitive tasks. Second, there is interest in the degree to which the introversion/ extroversion of the subject may make a difference. Third, there seems to be the issue of different types of music having different effects. There is an idea that sometimes music may hurt performance if it is too annoying or intrusive. This seems like a good start.

Abigail's literature on child welfare

Abigail has decided to look at child welfare supervisors and see if their particular supervisory skills predict client outcomes. She looks at the supervision literature, as supervisors seem to be an important link between workers and their organisations. These sources have shown Abigail a number of things. First of all, her area has been looked at, and there seems to be a person (Glisson) who is cited a lot and seems to be the main researcher in this area.

There has been work done on how organisational and supervisory factors affect workers, especially with regard to stress and burnout; and also a small amount has been done on how supervisory factors affect clients. Abigail now has to think about how she will narrow her question. The more she thinks about what she has found, the less interested she becomes. She finds herself wanting to look at something more tangible. As she is looking through the sources, one article in particular catches her eye:

This article interests her for a number of reasons: The field of client death seems to have some linkage to theory but appears understudied with regard to child welfare workers. It is in an area that Abigail understands, and there seem to be practical implications surrounding how child welfare workers handle the death of a child on their caseload. Does it lead to them quitting? Do they become less effective if they don't deal with it well? Although most of the literature seems to look at helping professionals in general, it seems that child welfare might be a special case because child welfare workers are specifically charged with the safety of their child clients as their primary focus and make critical decisions regarding their safety on a daily basis.

Furthermore, fatalities on child welfare worker caseloads are likely to be homicides, whereas many psychotherapeutic caseload deaths are suicides. Finally, the agency that Abigail worked for was interested in this issue. She seems to recall them having some kind of training on it. Perhaps they would be interested in hosting the research?

As a result of her literature review, Abigail has now decided to radically switch her focus to child fatalities and how workplace and other factors are associated with better or worse worker outcomes. She thinks that she will have to look at work environment and the worker's home environment and see how these correlate with either better or worse functioning following the death of the child client. Admittedly, this is still somewhat fuzzy, but Abigail hopes it will come together a little bit better in the design phase.

Reviewing the Field

We have looked at the academic literature, but if our work is going to be practically relevant, we need to know more about what is actually going on in the community. If you are doing basic science, then you may skip this part altogether. Many times, people come to an area of interest because they have some field experience and so are already familiar with how their issues play out in practice. Sometimes, however, people decide they want to look at an issue that is new to them and about which they know basically nothing.

In the world of social science, there are few things as frightening as a researcher using standardised instruments and sophisticated statistics to study an area he or she knows nothing about in a practical sense. In the end, though, there is really no substitute for experience. Is it possible for you to contact someone who does the work you are interested in? Can you buy that person lunch and get feedback about your ideas? Is there anything like a "ride-along" available in your area of interest? Once you settle on an area of career interest, the best alternative is for you to work or volunteer in the area, even if it is for only a few hours per week.

There is really no substitute for having experience working with the population you study. If you don't have such experience, we strongly recommend you get some. Among our examples, John has had experience working with Bosnians at a refugee service centre, but he doesn't know much about the community otherwise. As a next step, John decides to find out about local agencies serving Bosnian refugees. His school's practicum office knows of several supervisors who work in these agencies, and the Assistant Director of Field knows one personally.

John uses this contact to get in touch with this person, invites her to lunch, and is able to quickly pick up an introduction to the Bosnian social service scene in his town. It mostly revolves around the Resettlement House, a local service centre for refugees that serves several hundred Bosnians.

John now has at least a general idea of what science is being done and what agencies are working with the population in his area. He also decides to broaden his knowledge of the population by reading what he can find about them, attending cultural events hosted by the community, and starting to do some volunteer work at the Resettlement House. He still has not specified his question, and isn't sure what theories will guide him. This is his next task.

Abigail talks to her old supervisor and finds that there may be a great deal of receptiveness at the county, or maybe even the state, level to doing a study of workers who have had clients die. She is excited about the opportunity to do research within a system she knows so well. Maria decides that she can make better sense of communities and violence by talking to police officers.

She decides to do a number of ride-alongs in poor and in wealthy areas. This enables her to both get a better sense for the people and events in these neighbourhoods and to get feedback from police about their perspectives on what goes on and why. Yuan, while not as experienced as Abigail, does understand how work is done at his agency. His biggest need is to understand the specific intervention being tested, CBT, and how it may be used in other agencies. It might be useful for him to contact people at other agencies who use the model and find out more about the issues that have arisen in their experience. Professor Kathy is doing work that has practical application only to professors and research assistants. She already knows all about that, so she does nothing special to learn more.

Understanding Your Literature

After your initial literature review, you need to check to see that you can answer the following questions:

1. What questions have been asked by others in my area?
2. What populations have been studied and at what level (i.e., individual, community, and so on)?
3. What constructs or variables have been looked at?
4. What instruments (tests) or other measures have been used in my area?
5. What theories exist to tell me how to think about my area or what relationships are likely to exist there?
6. What kinds of designs (experimental, correlational, and the like.) are used in my area?
7. What are the main empirical findings in my area?
8. What needs to be studied next in my area?

Your next task is to look at the literature you've got and try to see if you can answer the above questions. If you can't, then you need to go back and fill in the gaps with more literature. We will describe each of the above points in detail.

What Questions Have Been Asked by Others in My Area?

Perhaps the easiest question to answer is what research questions others have asked. Any competently written research article will tell you precisely what questions are being asked and how these questions build on prior work. Unless your area is brand new, you may notice that there will be clusters of studies that look at particular issues and reference each other.

Try to see what the big issues are in your area. Note carefully exactly how the questions in your literature are phrased and try to see if these questions make sense to you. A good question should be clear, testable, and meaningful. One problem that stops many of our students dead is that they can't find many articles relating to their precise question. If you can't find literature in your area, find literature about the closest thing possible.

For example, let's say you want to do a study where you try to raise the self-confidence and improve the self-image of very young amputees (4 to 6 years old). Let's say you can't find much on it. What you would do is go to the literature on adolescent or adult amputees and their adjustment and see what you could find there. You would also go to the developmental literature on young children and see what that would contribute to your work. Possibly there is a parallel literature that you could tap. Nobody is going to blame you for broadening your sources if there is no alternative. In short, if you can't find it, find the next closest thing.

Understanding what the questions in your area are allows you some room for creativity and critical thought. Do the questions make sense to you? Are they studied in a way that fits with what you know from your experiences in the field? Are there questions that are not asked but that strike you as critical? Time spent thinking about these things is time well spent.

What Populations Have Been Studied, and at What Level?

Researchers often focus on particular groups of people

for no scientifically valid reason. For example, college freshmen are not typical Americans, but vast amounts of research have been done only on them, just because they're available. Some fields (psychology) have been criticised for focusing almost exclusively on middleclass Whites. Other kinds of work, such as poverty studies, have spent quite a lot of effort on some populations (poor inner-city residents) while largely ignoring other groups (the rural poor).

You should use your common sense and see if the questions being asked match well with the populations studied. Are racial, class, sexual orientation, gender, and other critical forms of diversity within our population being well covered? What are the units of analysis in the studies you reviewed?

Most studies use individuals as the unit of analysis, but other levels, including families, groups, organisations, census tracts, zip codes, cities, counties, or states are used. Sometimes the unit of analysis is a measure of time, such as a day.We recently submitted a grant in which we counted the number of violent events each day in a four-year period in an attempt to try to understand the degree to which violent sporting events might be associated with rises in violent acts. Ask yourself what level your question has been explored on, and see if you can think of other ways to look at your issue at different levels of analysis.

What Constructs and Variables Have Been Looked At?

Constructs are the things we study. When we look at them in a highly operationalised form, we call them variables. In this sense, depression might be the construct you want to study, but you may operationalise depression as the subject's score on the Beck Depression Inventory. The score from that scale is now your variable representing depression. Sometimes researchers get clumsy or lazy or just plain do bad work, and you may find yourself easily confused.

For example, many studies will list "mental health" as an outcome, but will measure only subject depression. This is not a global measure of "mental health" at all, just of a single part of it. Other times, a researcher may operationalise "job exit" as the person's stated intention to leave the job, while another researcher may operationalise the same construct as the actual exit. These are very different.

You should be familiar with the constructs and variables in your area. Do they include the things you want to study? Do you agree with how constructs are turned into variables? Is some key construct or variable missing? Do the constructs apply well to the people you want to study? There may also be considerable debate in a given area regarding the appropriate construct or variable to use.

For example, Papadopoulos and Lee point out that there are yet to be agreed-upon means of measuring or controlling for culture across studies and disciplines. Berry and colleagues detail several aspects of culture that one might consider in research. Further, one should always check out constructs with members of the population to be studied. Different cultures may have very different ways of defining and discussing various concepts of interest.

What Instruments (Tests) or Other Measures Are Used?

Most studies have very specific ways of measuring variables of interest. This will commonly take the form of a score on a test. Sometimes there will be broad agreement about how to measure something. For example, the Beck Depression Inventory we mentioned above is very commonly used for measuring depression, while the CBCL (Child Behaviour Checklist) is commonly used to measure children's emotional and behavioural problems. Instruments have different strengths and weaknesses.

To stay with the example of the Beck Depression Inventory: This instrument gives you a continuous score, which is very useful for most statistical analyses, but it does not tell you other things. If, for example, you want to know if someone meets the current diagnostic criteria for depression, then you can't use the Beck, because it does not conform to diagnostic criteria for depression as found in the Diagnostic and Statistical Manual of Mental Disorders (DSM-IV-TR).

You want something like depression section from the DIS-IV (Diagnostic Interview Schedule - IV), an instrument designed to test whether or not someone meets DSM-IV-TR diagnostic criteria. You need to have a pretty clear understanding of what instruments exist to study the constructs you are interested in. The best way to do this is simply to see what others have used. We would also recommend the Mental Measurements Yearbook site.

Another good resource specific to children and youth is Conducting School- Based Assessments of Child and Adolescent Behaviour. Finally one must consider whether or not a given measure has been used with your population. There may be cultural biases in instruments due to conceptual differences, linguistic issues, or other problems. The New Handbook of Multicultural Assessment: Clinical, Psychological, and Educational Applications is a great resource for helping you to understand if a measure is culturally appropriate.

What Relationships Are Likely to Exist in My Data?

Understanding what theories to use and how to use them

is very important. It is also probably the most difficult part of the entire research process. The role of theory in your work will depend entirely on the issue you are interested in studying. Just like understanding variables or instruments, a good place to start with theory is to see what other people are using. It is not plagiarism or copying to base your work on the work of others. It is how science works. We call this "knowledge building."What you can't do is take credit for the work of others.

Right now your task is to find out about the theories that are important in your area. Good articles will overview the theories on which their design is based. It shouldn't be too difficult to see what theories are commonly used or even dominant in your area. For example, in the treatment of phobias, you will quickly find that many studies test behavioural or cognitive behavioural treatments.

You will find relatively few studies on phobias examining the efficacy of treatments based in humanistic theory. As in the other areas, you need to think for yourself here. Do the theories match up with the research populations, questions, and designs in a clear way? It will almost certainly be necessary to go back to the literature and find more sources on the theories that are most commonly used or most appropriate to you.

What Kinds of Designs Are Used in My Area?

This will make more sense to you later, but try to figure out how people are doing research on your subject. Do they all use experimental designs? Do any of the articles you have found say they are "longitudinal"? Are qualitative methods used? Try to get a sense for what ways that researchers are approaching the area, so you can approach your own design with some background and the benefit of the prior work of others. You probably aren't at a place where you can really critically figure all this out yet, but don't worry, we'll get there.

What Are the Main Empirical Findings in My Area?

It can be confusing just listing out the findings from each article you read. Try to figure out what the big and consistent findings are. Which findings come up over and over again? Which hypotheses are consistently supported or are consistently not supported? Are there strong trends that generalise over time and across populations? Try to get a sense for the larger and more important empirical findings in your area.

Try to determine if the findings in your area represent large and meaningful differences, or if they simply report small effects that barely manage to reach statistical significance. For example, many studies find that boys are five or ten times as likely to become delinquent as girls. This is a big difference that matters. Other studies have found that birth order may influence IQ by a point or two. This is a small difference that has no practical importance.

You ought to be able to describe the findings in your area in simple terms. You should be able to say things like "The literature consistently reports a strong relationship between X and Y," or "We have reports only of weak or nonsignificant associations between X and Y." Don't panic, we'll teach you all about things like association and significance as we go forward. For now, just try to get a sense of what your literature says.

What Needs to Be Studied Next in My Area?

This is an easy one. Most articles end with a paragraph or so that tells the reader what kinds of research need to be done in the future. Simply go to the articles you have found and read what the authors have to say. Dissertations can be particularly good for this. This is another place to use your creativity. Start with these questions:

- What key questions are unanswered?
- What issues have been raised recently that need answering?
- What policies, events, or changes in the world suggest a new slant on the research?
- Have all important populations been studied with regard to your question?
- What strikes you as missing or important to look at?

Understanding the Literature

We will now look at our five friends and see how they are doing with regard to these issues.

- *John.* John has found a decently sized literature on Bosnians. In order to find out what form his research should take, he'd like to find some important gaps in the current work that he can exploit. Two themes have emerged. First, it is obvious to John that PTSD was getting all the attention. Second, there seems to be a real lack of any focus on strengths in the literature. As far as researchers are concerned, the issue is mental health (meaning PTSD), and that seems to be that. While John was originally planning to focus his work on PTSD, the lack of research in other key areas is too tempting to miss. So John searches for strengths or resiliency among Bosnian refugees and finds almost nothing except some qualitative descriptions of services that had been provided from a strengths perspective. John is starting to think that finding out more about the strengths of the Bosnians and how these strengths help in supporting mental health and economic success might be interesting, important, understudied, and fundable. More in-depth review of his sources brought up some interesting findings in this regard. Nesdale and Mak found that psychological health was higher among refugees with higher levels of personal achievement in their new cultures. Miller and colleagues found that lack of mastery in a range of areas was among the primary issues faced by Bosnian refugees in Chicago. A very common finding is represented by Baker who mastery of language most important things in adapting to life in America. How should John look at this strength stuff? He has no idea and needs some theory. One of his identified sources is a large book that seems as though it might have a nice theory review section. From this source, he identified two possible theoretical models to use and found that Berry and Kim's model seemed like a good fit. That model discussed four different types of acculturation and related them to mental health outcomes. John is beginning to believe that he would like to use this model, in conjunction with a focus on strengths, to look at different kinds of mental health and economic outcomes among Bosnian refugees.

— *Abigail.* Abigail has chosen to look at how client death affects child welfare workers. She is beginning to thing she is interested mainly in how client death may or may not lead to more or less trauma for different workers. From her readings, she has found that both a positive work environment and social support from family and friends should be helpful factors. As far as she can tell, there has been no empirical work to date looking at child welfare workers and their response to client fatality, but she does have models she can draw from that have been developed with populations of medical professionals.

- *Maria.* Maria has found theoretical reasons why she would expect homicide and suicide rates to be higher in some zip codes as well as a modest number of studies, mainly at the county or higher levels, showing how this is done empirically. Maria is in a good position at this point because the census variables available to her will allow her to track most of the things that interest her (poverty, housing, age, race, and the like), and her level of analysis (zip code) will provide her with better (finer level) data than have been previously found at the county level.
- *Yuan.* Yuan has found both theoretical and empirical sources that pertain to CBT and domestic violence. If anything, he has too many possible paths open to him, especially in the area of constructs and variables of interest. He has a range of outcome variables he can choose from, including a number of scales measuring various kinds of conflict or violence. He also has the option of studying events, ranging from perpetrator or spousal accounts of violence to a review of police records (if he can get them). The particular form of CBT to be used by Yuan's agency has a heavy emphasis on blocking violent behaviour through teaching alternate means of conflict resolution, so some measure that looks at how the family handles conflict, and how it changes over time, would seem logical.
- *Professor Kathy.* Professor Kathy just wants to know if playing music cuts down on errors. She is going to minimise the role of theory in her work and test just the expected relationship. This is because she doesn't care at all why music might reduce errors,

she just wants to see if it does. Based on her review of the literature, it looks as though she will want to use some kind of easy-listening or classical music, because music that is more modern might be intrusive or distracting. Her key concepts are listening to nonintrusive music and performance in research coding tasks. Her population is going to be her research assistants. Her overall goal is to see if she (and other researchers) should use background music for her coders.

Ethical Issues for Our Sample Projects

There are no ethical issues at this stage that prevent the researchers from going forward with their questions of interest. In other words, none of them are proposing something so dangerous to them or so potentially harmful to subjects or so unimportant as to be a waste of resources. There will be, however, ethical considerations for our researchers as they move forward into the design of their study. These will be dealt with in detail in subsequent chapters but are overviewed here.

Maria will be using data at the zip code level from the census, assuming that similar aggregate data can be found for suicide and homicide. Her study involves little human subjects consideration, low resources, and is important. If she uses only publicly available data, then she will have no concerns about confidentiality. John will have to carefully consider potential vulnerability due to immigration status, the sensitivity of the questions he will ask, how to address issues if a subject seems to need services, and confidentiality.

It will be important for John to get to know more about the culture and the local population. Finding a local leader and discussing the issue will be an important next step. Abigail's sample will be dealing with a traumatic issue, so care will be required to have a counselor or other resources available to support subjects who may have negative reactions. It will need to be made clear to subjects that their employment will in no way be affected by their decision to participate and that their employers will not be given access to confidential data.

Yuan's topic is important, and the agency is likely to support access to a sample. One concern is that he may be studying mandated clients, and they may potentially feel coerced into participating. Because recidivism is a harmful occurrence for the partner of the subjects as well as the clients, it is especially important that the study must not include withholding treatment that would otherwise have been provided. Kathy has already selected a nonintrusive form of music, is sampling adults, and is not asking potentially harmful questions. She will just have to insure that students are not feeling pressured to participate due to grades or fearful of termination of a job as a research assistant. She might also have to consider possible stress reactions to the task.

Conceptual Framework

This is where you move from simply reporting what others have said to more carefully defining your personal area of interest. We use the term conceptual framework to mean what constructs and relationships you are interested in, how they might fit together, whom you are interested in, and what theories underlie your work.

Students (and most professors) typically jump to the "how" of design before they understand the constructs they are studying (what), their population of interest (who) and the practical issues and theories underlying their work (why). This leads, almost without exception, to people who don't really understand what they're doing. This results in people having bad experiences and needing to go back to the proverbial drawing board.

Constructs

Constructs are the things we study. They can be almost anything, from traits to opinions to events to treatment interventions to virtually anything you can think of. They all share several things in common, though. Usable constructs are easy to understand and specific and can be transformed into variables that are clearly operationalised and measured. Constructs can be concrete things, like weight, or they can be more conceptual, like "depression."

The less clear and specific your constructs are, the more work you will have to do in transforming them into measurable variables. Ideally, constructs should also have practical importance. Just as all questions are not equally important, all constructs are not equally important. For example, hunger was a serious social problem in the United States 50 years ago. It is a less critical issue today. Even among the very poor, obesity is probably a far greater threat to health than hunger. Concepts relating to poor nutrition would be a far more important thing to measure than low caloric intake, at least in the United States.

Relationships between constructs are the things we test in our models. Many of the relationships between constructs are so obvious that you might not even notice them. For example, anyone studying delinquency is likely to understand that the construct of gender is strongly related to delinquency. Relationships between constructs are a big part of what social science is all about. You are probably not very interested in just measuring your constructs in isolation but instead want to know how they relate to something.

The big issue is this: How do you know what relationships to look for? This is where theory comes in. There may be any number of theories relating to your constructs. These theories may describe how your construct develops or is caused (etiology), how it is spread across society (epidemiology), and what other constructs are related to it. You must know these theories. The relationships you will be looking for will come from them. If you cannot show how the relationships you are exploring or testing are derived from or related to theory, your work may not be taken seriously.

Sometimes your area is so new that there is little theory present. In these cases, your work will probably be mainly descriptive or exploratory and inductive. However, you still need some kind of theoretical framework to specify what you want to describe. You never just go charging out with nothing in your head. It just isn't possible. Your reasons for choosing to look at what you look at in a descriptive study are probably based on some general perspective, such as a systems approach or a developmental approach. In such a case, go ahead and state that your work is being done under the general theoretical orientation you choose and discuss how this orientation shapes your work.

Specification and Ethical Concerns

Your conceptual framework must reference whom or what you are studying. This includes a description of the people, organisations, or whatever that you will be including in your research. You need to explain clearly how the populations you include in your conceptual framework are appropriate to the constructs you have chosen and the theory you are using. For example, many studies have been criticised for using only easily available populations. College students are common subjects, but this might not help you find out about the population as a whole.

A serious ethical concern is the underrepresentation of women and minorities in the literature, which was especially serious in decades past. People applying for grants to many federal agencies are required to write special sections that explain how the proposed research will sample and apply to a broad range of people. This is so that the benefits of the work can be shared by all kinds of people. There are exceptions to this, obviously. If you are studying something that mainly affects one type of person, then it is reasonable to include only the people to whom that issue pertains. Furthermore, you may have theoretical reasons for only sampling one segment of the population.

Parsimony

Parsimony is a ten-buck word for "simplicity." We are all familiar with the advice, "Keep It Simple, Stupid," often abbreviated as KISS. This applies to conceptual models just as it does to most things in life. You can achieve parsimony in your model by doing the following:

How to be parsimonious

Limit the number of constructs: Just include those constructs that you expect will have meaningfully large effects on the model. If income was previously shown to account for 1% of the variance in what you're studying you probably should leave it out of the model.

Include Only Relationships That You Have Good Theoretical Reason For or That Other Studies Have Found in the Past: It is tempting to say, "Gee, maybe everything relates to everything! Let's see!" This is bad. A model that specifies (draws lines for) all possible relationships between constructs is "saturated" and can cause some statistical analysis programmes to refuse to run.

Your model must reflect your best judgment about the most important relationships you hope to find. Warning: Later we will use again use the word saturated in the qualitative analysis chapter. Saturated has two totally different meanings in research. A saturated theoretical model is bad, but reaching saturation in a qualitative analysis is good. Sorry about that.

Does this mean you must always use the simplest possible model? Absolutely not. In the above example, the diagram on the left is very heavily specified: If that's what theory or evidence suggests is best, however, you may have to sacrifice some parsimony. Your models don't have to be parsimonious, but you should have a darn good explanation for why they aren't.

Example Projects- Conceptual Frameworks

Let's have a look at the conceptual frameworks for our five sample cases.

— *John.* John is interested in the constructs of strengths and acculturation. He has found relatively little on this, however, and feels that he should start his research by consulting the Bosnians themselves and getting their perspective. He believes that he may therefore be pursuing a more qualitative approach. Because John is planning to go into the community and get the perspectives of the people he is studying, he feels he should allow them considerable scope in defining strengths. As for acculturation outcomes, he is planning on seeing how well Berry and Kim's model will serve as a framework for understanding what the Bosnians have to say about their own experience. This model specifies four different acculturation outcomes. These are assimilation, in which an immigrant abandons his or her prior culture and becomes Americanised;

integration, in which the immigrant maintains parts of his or her culture but also joins with the American culture; separation, in which the immigrant retains his or her culture entirely and rejects American culture; and marginalisation, an early stage in the process in which the conflict and crisis of immigration cause the person to be isolated from both his or her culture and American culture. John expects that he will find that the Bosnians he talks to will be able to give him information on what strengths lead to more positive acculturation outcomes (integration) and relatively rapid transition through marginalisation. He expects his subjects will report a lack of strengths to be associated with separation and extended marginalisation. John expects to find local Bosnian immigrants and interview them, either individually or in groups. He intends to give them wide latitude in how they respond, but he also wants to get his core questions answered.

— *Abigail.* The more Abigail thinks about it, the more she realises that her question might best be phrased "Are environmental (work, family, friends) factors associated with different responses to child fatality among child welfare workers?" She consulted a reference book of psychological tests and has found some measures that look like they might be helpful in capturing her constructs of interest and answering her theoretical questions. These include the following:

  — *The Impact of Events Scale (IES),* by M. Horowitz, produces two subscales measuring bad psychological outcomes of a traumatic event. These include intrusive experiences (can't stop thinking about the event, bad dreams, and the like) and avoidance (trying not to think about the event, avoiding places that make you remember it, and so on).

- *The Social Support Behaviours Scale (SSB),* by A. Vaux, S. Reidel, and D. Stewart, measures five different kinds of social support. Abigail is especially interested in the subscales on emotional support and advice/guidance.
- *The Organisational Climate Scale (OCS)* by A. Thompson and H. McCubbin measures various aspects of organisational climate as perceived by the respondent.

It seems to Abigail that these scales will let her capture many of the key constructs that her literature review cited as important. There will be a number of other constructs she may also want to measure, but the IES appears to be a good dependent measure, and the SSB and the OCS seem to provide a range of key environmental predictor factors.

- *Maria.* Maria's constructs are homicide and suicide (in San Diego zip codes) and community characteristics. She expects crowded housing and low income to be associated with both suicide and homicide. Her population will be the population of San Diego County but aggregated at zip code level.
- *Yuan.* Yuan is interested in the concept of different treatment types (CBT versus treatment as usual) and how they are associated with conflict strategies and violence. He will test to see if either type of treatment has clearly better outcomes. His population is determined for him and will be people using his agency's services.
- *Professor Kathy.* Kathy will look at nonintrusive music and see if it improves correct coding by her researchers.

FORMALISING AND PRESENTING YOUR CONCEPTUAL FRAMEWORK

In communicating your conceptual framework to others, you will have to be able to present your ideas in a clear manner using terms that others will understand. To do this, you will have to know the terms we use to describe variables, and you will need to know how to graphically represent your conceptual framework so that others can see an understand it. We will start out by becoming a little more technical in how we discuss variables. Variables are operationalised constructs.

But what does operationalised mean? Something is operationalised if it is clear how it is measured. For example, "suicide attempt history" is not operationalised, but "number of prior suicide attempts reported by the subject during the interview" is operationalised. There are lots of ways to operationalise constructs.

Types of Scales for Variables

There are four different ways in which variables may be scaled to represent their constructs: nominal, ordinal, interval, and ratio. If you know French, you can remember this by the fact that the first letter of each scale (in the above order) spells Noir, the French word for "black" (as in "film noir").

— *Nominal scales* (categorical) are just names or types that have no numerical significance. "Blond," "Republican," "Joan," and "Female" are nominal.

— *Ordinal scales* (categorical) are not common in social research and relate to the rank order something has. For example, a ranking of the worst earthquakes in terms of fatalities (most killed, second most killed, and so on) and Olympic medals (first, second, third) are ordinal variables. Notice that these are numeric only in the sense that you know who came first and second; you do not know how much difference there was between them. For example, the winner of the 500 meter freestyle may have beaten the second place person by only .01 second, while the second place person beat the third place person by a whopping 9 seconds, but they're still listed as "first, second, third."

- *Interval scales* (continuous) are different from ordinal variables in that the differences between numbers are the same. If we record the temperature each day on the Fahrenheit scale, then we are recording numbers where the difference between each number on our scale is the same (one degree). Interval scales lack "true zeros" (see the following).
- *Ratio scales* (continuous) are like interval scales but have "true zeros." A true zero is when a value of zero means that the amount being measured is nothing.

Categorical and Continuous Variables

Variables measured with nominal or ordinal scales are generally called "categorical variables." Variables measured with ratio or interval scales are called "continuous variables" because the difference between each point on the scale is the same. Many statistics require that your variables be continuous. One confusing point is that most researchers treat scores from psychological or similar tests as continuous, even when there is no reason to really believe that they are, if you use a strict definition.

Independent, Control, and Dependent Variables

- *Independent variables* can be though of as "predictor" or "causal" variables. Independent variables are those things you believe will predict or cause a change in the dependent variable. When drawing models, independent variables are to the left.

- *Dependent variables* can be thought of as "outcome" variables. They are those things you believe are affected by other things in your model. When drawing models, the independent variable is the item furthest to the right. There are also "mediating" and "moderating" variables, which we will discuss below.
- *Control variables* are other possible influences on your dependent variable that you decide to keep track of. They are included in your model to make sure that the relationship between independent and dependent variables is not due to other factors.

2

Philosophy of Social Research

All research is based on assumptions about how the world is perceived and how we can best come to understand it. Of course, nobody really knows how we can best understand the world, and philosophers have been arguing about that very question for at least two millennia now, so all we're going to do is look at how most contemporary social scientists approach the question of how we know about the world around us. We consider two major philosophical schools of thought—Positivism and Post-Positivism—that are especially important perspectives for contemporary social research.

Research Structure

Most research projects share the same general structure. You might think of this structure as following the shape of an hourglass. The research process usually starts with a broad area of interest, the initial problem that the researcher wishes to study. For instance, the researcher could be interested in how to use computers to improve the performance of students in mathematics. But this initial interest is far too broad to study in any single research project (it might not even be addressable in a lifetime of research).

The researcher has to narrow the question down to one that can reasonably be studied in a research project. This might involve formulating a hypothesis or a focus question. For instance, the researcher might hypothesize that a particular method of computer instruction in math will improve the ability of elementary school students in a specific district. At the narrowest point of the research hourglass, the researcher is engaged in direct measurement or observation of the question of interest.

Once the basic data is collected, the researcher begins to try to understand it, usually by analysing it in a variety of ways. Even for a single hypothesis there are a number of analyses a researcher might typically conduct. At this point, the researcher begins to formulate some initial conclusions about what happened as a result of the computerised math programme. Finally, the researcher often will attempt to address the original broad question of interest by generalising from the results of this specific study to other related situations. For instance, on the basis of strong results indicating that the math programme had a positive effect on student performance, the researcher might conclude that other school districts similar to the one in the study might expect similar results.

Components of a Research Study

What are the basic components or parts of a research study? Here, we'll describe the basic components involved in a causal study. Because causal studies presuppose descriptive and relational questions, many of the components of causal studies will also be found in those others. Most social research originates from some general problem or question. You might, for instance, be interested in what programmes enable the unemployed to get jobs. Usually, the problem is broad enough that you could not hope to address it adequately in a single research study. Consequently, we typically narrow the problem down to a more specific research question that we can hope to address.

The research question is often stated in the context of some theory that has been advanced to address the problem. For instance, we might have the theory that ongoing support services are needed to assure that the newly employed remain employed. The research question is the central issue being addressed in the study and is often phrased in the language of theory. For instance, a research question might be:

Is a programme of supported employment more effective (than no programme at all) at keeping newly employed persons on the job? The problem with such a question is that it is still too general to be studied directly. Consequently, in most research we develop an even more specific statement. For instance, the hypothesis for the employment study might be something like:

The Metropolitan Supported Employment Programme will significantly increase rates of employment after six months for persons who are newly employed (after being out of work for at least one year) compared with persons who receive no comparable programme. Notice that this hypothesis is specific enough that a reader can understand quite well what the study is trying to assess.

In causal studies, we have at least two major variables of interest, the cause and the effect. Usually the cause is some type of event, programme, or treatment. We make a distinction between causes that the researcher can control (such as a programme) versus causes that occur naturally or outside the researcher's influence (such as a change in interest rates, or the occurrence of an earthquake).

The effect is the outcome that you wish to study. For both the cause and effect we make a distinction between the idea of them (the construct) and how they are actually manifested in reality. For instance, when we think about what a programme of support services for the newly employed might be, we are thinking of the "construct." On the other hand, the real world is not always what we think it is. In research, we remind ourselves of this by distinguishing the view of an entity (the construct) from the entity as it exists (the operationalisation). Ideally, we would like the two to agree.

Social research is always conducted in a social context. We ask people questions, or observe families interacting, or measure the opinions of people in a city. An important component of a research project is the units that participate in the project. Units are directly related to the question of sampling. In most projects we cannot involve all of the people we might like to involve. For instance, in studying a programme of support services for the newly employed we can't possibly include in the study everyone in the world, or even in the country, who is newly employed. Instead, we have to try to obtain a representative sample of such people.

When sampling, we make a distinction between the theoretical population of interest to the study and the final sample that we actually measure in the study. Usually the term "units" refers to the people that we sample and from whom we gather information. But for some projects the units are organisations, groups, or geographical entities like cities or towns. Sometimes the sampling strategy is multi-level: we sample a number of cities and within them sample families.

In causal studies, we are interested in the effects of some cause on one or more outcomes. The outcomes are directly related to the research problem—we are usually most interested in outcomes that are most reflective of the problem. In the hypothetical supported employment study, we would probably be most interested in measures of employment—is the person currently employed, or, what is their rate of absenteeism.

Finally, in a causal study we usually are comparing the effects of the cause of interest (e.g., the programme) relative to other conditions (e.g., another programme or no programme at all). Thus, a key component in a causal study concerns how we decide what units (e.g., people) receive the programme and which are placed in an alternative condition. This issue is directly related to the research design that we use in the study. One of the central questions in research design is determining how people wind up in or are placed in various programmes or treatments that we are comparing.

These, then, are the major components in a causal study:

— The Research Problem

— The Research Question

— The Programme (Cause)

— The Units

— The Outcomes (Effect)

— The Design

Deduction and Induction

Deductive and Inductive Thinking

Deductive reasoning works from the more general to the more specific. Sometimes this is informally called a "top-down" approach. We might begin with thinking up a theory about the topic of interest. We then narrow that down into more specific hypotheses that we can test. We narrow down even further when we collect observations to address the hypotheses. This ultimately leads us to be able to test the hypotheses with specific data—a confirmation (or not) of the original theories.

Inductive reasoning works the other way, moving from specific observations to broader generalisations and theories. Informally, we sometimes call this a "bottom up" approach (please note that it's "bottom up" and not "bottoms up" which is the kind of thing the bartender says to customers when he's trying to close for the night!). In inductive reasoning, we begin with specific observations and measures, begin to detect patterns and regularities, formulate some tentative hypotheses that we can explore, and finally end up developing some general conclusions or theories.

These two methods of reasoning have a very different "feel" to them when you're conducting research. Inductive reasoning, by its very nature, is more open-ended and exploratory, especially at the beginning. Deductive reasoning is more narrow in nature and is concerned with testing or confirming hypotheses. Even though a particular study may look like it's purely deductive (e.g., an experiment designed to test the hypothesized effects of some treatment on some outcome), most social research involves both inductive and deductive reasoning processes at some time in the project.

In fact, it doesn't take a rocket scientist to see that we could assemble the two graphs above into a single circular one that continually cycles from theories down to observations and back up again to theories. Even in the most constrained experiment, the researchers may observe patterns in the data that lead them to develop new theories.

Positivism and Post-Positivism

The term epistemology comes from the Greek word

episteme, their term for knowledge. In simple terms, epistemology is the philosophy of knowledge or of how we come to know. Methodology is also concerned with how we come to know, but is much more practical in nature. Methodology is focused on the specific ways—the methods—that we can use to try to understand the world better.

Epistemology and methodology are intimately related: the former involves the philosophy of how we come to know the world and the latter involves the practice. When most people in the society think about science, they think about some guy in a white lab coat working at a lab bench mixing up chemicals. They think of science as boring, cut-and-dry, and they think of the scientist as narrow-minded and esoteric (the ultimate nerd—think of the humorous but nonetheless mad scientist in the Back to the Future movies, for instance). A lot of the stereotypes about science come from a period where science was dominated by a particular philosophy—positivism—that tended to support some of these views.

Let's begin by considering what positivism is. In its broadest sense, positivism is a rejection of metaphysics. It is a position that holds that the goal of knowledge is simply to describe the phenomena that we experience. The purpose of science is simply to stick to what we can observe and measure. Knowledge of anything beyond that, a positivist would hold, is impossible. These were the mythical 'rat runners' who believed that psychology could only study what could be directly observed and measured.

Since we can't directly observe emotions, thoughts, etc. (although we may be able to measure some of the physical and physiological accompaniments), these were not legitimate topics for a scientific psychology. B.F. Skinner argued that psychology needed to concentrate only on the positive and negative reinforcers of behaviour in order to predict how people will behave—everything else in between (like what the person is thinking) is irrelevant because it can't be measured.

In a positivist view of the world, science was seen as the way to get at truth, to understand the world well enough so that we might predict and control it. The world and the universe were deterministic—they operated by laws of cause and effect that we could discern if we applied the unique approach of the scientific method. Science was largely a mechanistic or mechanical affair.

We use deductive reasoning to postulate theories that we can test. Based on the results of the studies, we may learn that the theory doesn't fit the facts well and so we need to revise the theory to better predict reality. The positivist believed in empiricism—the idea that observation and measurement was the core of the scientific endeavour. The key approach of the scientific method is the experiment, the attempt to discern natural laws through direct manipulation and observation.

A post-positivist might begin by recognising that the way scientists think and work and the way we think in the everyday life are not distinctly different. Scientific reasoning and common sense reasoning are essentially the same process. There is no difference in kind between the two, only a difference in degree. Scientists, for example, follow specific procedures to assure that observations are verifiable, accurate and consistent. In everyday reasoning, we don't always proceed so carefully.

One of the most common forms of post-positivism is a philosophy called critical realism. A critical realist believes that there is a reality independent of the thinking about it that science can study. (This is in contrast with a subjectivist who would hold that there is no external reality—we're each making this all up!). Positivists were also realists. The difference is that the post-positivist critical realist recognises that all observation is fallible and has error and that all theory is revisable.

In other words, the critical realist is critical of the ability to know reality with certainty. Where the positivist believed that the goal of science was to uncover the truth, the post-positivist critical realist believes that the goal of science is to hold steadfastly to the goal of getting it right about reality, even though we can never achieve that goal! Because all measurement is fallible, the post-positivist emphasizes the importance of multiple measures and observations, each of which may possess different types of error, and the need to use triangulation across these multiple errorful sources to try to get a better bead on what's happening in reality.

The post-positivist also believes that all observations are theory-laden and that scientists (and everyone else, for that matter) are inherently biased by their cultural experiences, world views, and so on. This is not cause to give up in despair, however. Post-positivism rejects the relativist idea of the incommensurability of different perspectives, the idea that we can never understand each other because we come from different experiences and cultures. Most post-positivists are constructivists who believe that we each construct the view of the world based on the perceptions of it. Because perception and observation is fallible, the constructions must be imperfect. So what is meant by objectivity in a post-positivist world? Positivists believed that objectivity was a characteristic that resided in the individual scientist.

Scientists are responsible for putting aside their biases and beliefs and seeing the world as it 'really' is. Post-positivists reject the idea that any individual can see the world perfectly as it really is. We are all biased and all of the observations are affected (theory-laden). The best hope for achieving objectivity is to triangulate across multiple fallible perspectives! Thus, objectivity is not the characteristic of an individual, it is inherently a social phenomenon. It is what multiple individuals are trying to achieve when they criticize each other's work. We never achieve objectivity perfectly, but we can approach it.

The best way for us to improve the objectivity of what we do is to do it within the context of a broader contentious community of truth-seekers (including other scientists) who criticize each other's work. The theories that survive such intense scrutiny are a bit like the species that survive in the evolutionary struggle. They have adaptive value and are probably as close as the species can come to being objective and understanding reality.

Define Validity

The first thing we have to ask is: "validity of what?" When we think about validity in research, most of us think about research components. We might say that a measure is a valid one, or that a valid sample was drawn, or that the design had strong validity. But all of those statements are technically incorrect. Measures, samples and designs don't 'have' validity—only propositions can be said to be valid. Technically, we should say that a measure leads to valid conclusions or that a sample enables valid inferences, and so on. It is a proposition, inference or conclusion that can 'have' validity.

We make lots of different inferences or conclusions while conducting research. Many of these are related to the process of doing research and are not the major hypotheses of the study. Nevertheless, like the bricks that go into building a wall, these intermediate process and methodological propositions provide the foundation for the substantive conclusions that we wish to address. For instance, virtually all social research involves measurement or observation. And, whenever we measure or observe we are concerned with whether we are measuring what we intend to measure or with how the observations are influenced by the circumstances in which they are made.

Subdivide validity into four types. Each type addresses a specific methodological question. In order to understand the types of validity. Because all four validity types are really only operative when studying causal questions.

There are really two realms that are involved in research. The first, is the land of theory. It is what goes on inside the heads as researchers. It is were we keep the theories about how the world operates. The second, is the land of observations. It is the real world into which we translate the ideas—our programmes, treatments, measures and observations. When we conduct research, we are continually flitting back and forth between these two realms, between what we think about the world and what is going on in it.

When we are investigating a cause-effect relationship, we have a theory (implicit or otherwise) of what the cause is (the cause construct). For instance, if we are testing a new educational programme, we have an idea of what it would look like ideally. Similarly, on the effect side, we have an idea of what we are ideally trying to affect and measure (the effect construct). But each of these, the cause and the effect, has to be translated into real things, into a programme or treatment and a measure or observational method. We use the term operationalisation to describe the act of translating a construct into its manifestation.

In effect, we take the idea and describe it as a series of operations or procedures. Now, instead of it only being an idea in the minds, it becomes a public entity that anyone can look at and examine for themselves. It is one thing, for instance, for you to say that you would like to measure self-esteem (a construct). But when you show a ten-item paper-and-pencil self-esteem measure that you developed for that purpose, others can look at it and understand more clearly what you intend by the term self-esteem.

Now, back to explaining the four validity types. Imagine that we wish to examine whether use of a World Wide Web (WWW) Virtual Classroom improves student understanding of course material. Assume that we took these two constructs, the cause construct (the WWW site) and the effect (understanding), and operationalised them—turned them into realities by constructing the WWW site and a measure of knowledge of the course material. Here are the four validity types and the question each addresses:

Conclusion Validity: In this study, is there a relationship between the two variables?: In the context of the example we're considering, the question might be worded: in this study, is there a relationship between the WWW site and knowledge of course material? There are several conclusions or inferences we might draw to answer such a question. We could, for example, conclude that there is a relationship. We might conclude that there is a positive relationship. We might infer that there is no relationship. We can assess the conclusion validity of each of these conclusions or inferences.

Internal Validity: Assuming that there is a relationship in this study, is the relationship a causal one?: Just because we find that use of the WWW site and knowledge are correlated, we can't necessarily assume that WWW site use causes the knowledge. Both could, for example, be caused by the same factor. For instance, it may be that wealthier students who have greater resources would be more likely to use have access to a WWW site and would excel on objective tests. When we want to make a claim that the programme or treatment caused the outcomes in the study, we can consider the internal validity of the causal claim.

Construct Validity: Assuming that there is a causal relationship in this study, can we claim that the programme reflected well the construct of the programme and that the measure reflected well the idea of the construct of the measure?: In simpler terms, did we implement the programme we intended to implement and did we measure the outcome we wanted to measure? In yet other terms, did we operationalise well the ideas of the cause and the effect? When the research is over, we would like to be able to conclude that we did a credible job of operationalising the constructs—we can assess the construct validity of this conclusion.

External Validity: Assuming that there is a causal relationship in this study between the constructs of the cause and the effect, can we generalise this effect to other persons, places or times?: We are likely to make some claims that the research findings have implications for other groups and individuals in other settings and at other times.

Notice how the question that each validity type addresses presupposes an affirmative answer to the previous one. This is what we mean when we say that the validity types build on one another. The figure shows the idea of cumulativeness as a staircase, along with the key question for each validity type.

For any inference or conclusion, there are always possible threats to validity—reasons the conclusion or inference might be wrong. Ideally, one tries to reduce the plausibility of the most likely threats to validity, thereby leaving as most plausible the conclusion reached in the study.

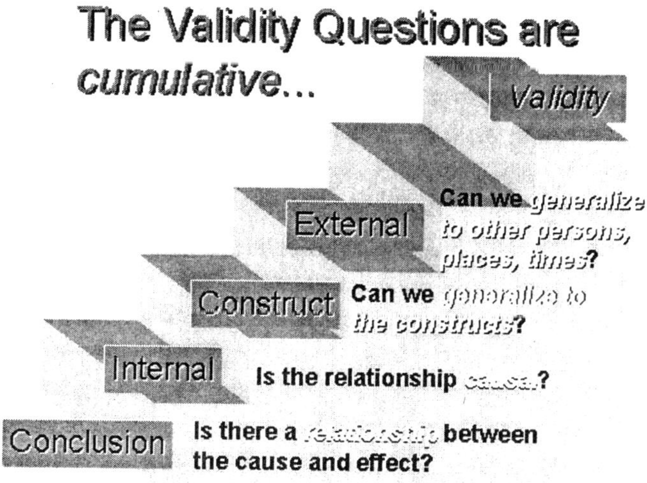

For instance, imagine a study examining whether there is a relationship between the amount of training in a specific technology and subsequent rates of use of that technology. Because the interest is in a relationship, it is considered an issue of conclusion validity.

Assume that the study is completed and no significant correlation between amount of training and adoption rates is found. On this basis it is concluded that there is no relationship between the two. How could this conclusion be wrong—that is, what are the "threats to validity"? For one, it's possible that there isn't sufficient statistical power to detect a relationship even if it exists. Perhaps the sample size is too small or the measure of amount of training is unreliable.

Or maybe assumptions of the correlational test are violated given the variables used. Perhaps there were random irrelevancies in the study setting or random heterogeneity in the respondents that increased the variability in the data and made it harder to see the relationship of interest.

The inference that there is no relationship will be stronger—have greater conclusion validity—if one can show that these alternative explanations are not credible. The distributions might be examined to see if they conform with assumptions of the statistical test, or analyses conducted to determine whether there is sufficient statistical power.

The theory of validity, and the many lists of specific threats, provide a useful scheme for assessing the quality of research conclusions. The theory is general in scope and applicability, well-articulated in its philosophical suppositions, and virtually impossible to explain adequately in a few minutes. As a framework for judging the quality of evaluations it is indispensable and well worth understanding.

Ethics in Research

We are going through a time of profound change in the understanding of the ethics of applied social research. From the time immediately after World War II until the early 1990s, there was a gradually developing consensus about the key ethical principles that should underlie the research endeavour. Two marker events stand out (among many others) as symbolic of this consensus. The Nuremberg War Crimes Trial following World War II brought to public view the ways German scientists had used captive human subjects as subjects in oftentimes gruesome experiments.

In the 1950s and 1960s, the Tuskegee Syphilis Study involved the withholding of known effective treatment for syphilis from African-American participants who were infected. Events like these forced the re-examination of ethical standards and the gradual development of a consensus that potential human subjects needed to be protected from being used as 'guinea pigs' in scientific research.

By the 1990s, the dynamics of the situation changed. Cancer patients and persons with AIDS fought publicly with the medical research establishment about the long time needed to get approval for and complete research into potential cures for fatal diseases.

In many cases, it is the ethical assumptions of the previous thirty years that drive this 'go-slow' mentality. After all, we would rather risk denying treatment for a while until we achieve enough confidence in a treatment, rather than run the risk of harming innocent people (as in the Nuremberg and Tuskegee events).

But now, those who were threatened with fatal illness were saying to the research establishment that they wanted to be test subjects, even under experimental conditions of considerable risk. You had several very vocal and articulate patient groups who wanted to be experimented on coming up against an ethical review system that was designed to protect them from being experimented on.

Although the last few years in the ethics of research have been tumultuous ones, it is beginning to appear that a new consensus is evolving that involves the stakeholder groups most affected by a problem participating more actively in the formulation of guidelines for research. While it's not entirely clear, at present, what the new consensus will be, it is almost certain that it will not fall at either extreme: protecting against human experimentation at all costs vs. allowing anyone who is willing to be experimented on.

Ethical Issues

There are a number of key phrases that describe the

system of ethical protections that the contemporary social and medical research establishment have created to try to protect better the rights of their research participants. The principle of voluntary participation requires that people not be coerced into participating in research. This is especially relevant where researchers had previously relied on 'captive audiences' for their subjects—prisons, universities, and places like that. Closely related to the notion of voluntary participation is the requirement of informed consent.

Essentially, this means that prospective research participants must be fully informed about the procedures and risks involved in research and must give their consent to participate. Ethical standards also require that researchers not put participants in a situation where they might be at risk of harm as a result of their participation. Harm can be defined as both physical and psychological. There are two standards that are applied in order to help protect the privacy of research participants.

Almost all research guarantees the participants confidentiality—they are assured that identifying information will not be made available to anyone who is not directly involved in the study. The stricter standard is the principle of anonymity which essentially means that the participant will remain anonymous throughout the study—even to the researchers themselves. Clearly, the anonymity standard is a stronger guarantee of privacy, but it is sometimes difficult to accomplish, especially in situations where participants have to be measured at multiple time points (e.g., a pre-post study). Increasingly, researchers have had to deal with the ethical issue of a person's right to service.

Good research practice often requires the use of a no-treatment control group—a group of participants who do not get the treatment or programme that is being studied. But when that treatment or programme may have beneficial effects, persons assigned to the no-treatment control may feel their rights to equal access to services are being curtailed.

Even when clear ethical standards and principles exist, there will be times when the need to do accurate research runs up against the rights of potential participants. No set of standards can possibly anticipate every ethical circumstance. Furthermore, there needs to be a procedure that assures that researchers will consider all relevant ethical issues in formulating research plans. To address such needs most institutions and organisations have formulated an Institutional Review Board (IRB), a panel of persons who reviews grant proposals with respect to ethical implications and decides whether additional actions need to be taken to assure the safety and rights of participants. By reviewing proposals for research, IRBs also help to protect both the organisation and the researcher against potential legal implications of neglecting to address important ethical issues of participants.

Conceptualising

One of the most difficult aspects of research—and one of the least discussed—is how to develop the idea for the research project in the first place. In training students, most faculty just assume that if you read enough of the research in an area of interest, you will somehow magically be able to produce sensible ideas for further research. Now, that may be true. And heaven knows that's the way we've been doing this higher education thing for some time now. One thing we can do (and some texts at least cover this at a surface level) is to give students a better idea of how professional researchers typically generate research ideas. Some of this is introduced in the discussion of problem formulation in applied social research.

But maybe we can do even better than that. Why can't we turn some of the expertise in developing methods into methods that students and researchers can use to help them formulate ideas for research. This approach, called concept mapping can be used by research teams to help them clarify and map out the key research issues in an area, to help them operationalise the programmes or interventions or the outcome measures for their study. The concept mapping method isn't the only method around that might help researchers formulate good research problems and projects. Virtually any method that's used to help individuals and groups to think more effectively would probably be useful in research formulation.

Some of the methods that might be included in the toolkit for research formulation might be: brainstorming, brainwriting, nominal group technique, focus groups, Delphi methods, and facet theory. And then, of course, there are all of the methods for identifying relevant literature and previous research work. If you know of any techniques or methods that you think might be useful when formulating the research problem, please feel free to add a notation—if there's a relevant Website, please point to it in the notation.

Problem Formulation

So how do researchers come up with the idea for a research project? Probably one of the most common sources of research ideas is the experience of practical problems in the field. Many researchers are directly engaged in social, health or human service programme implementation and come up with their ideas based on what they see happening around them. Others aren't directly involved in service contexts, but work with (or survey) people who are in order to learn what needs to be better understood.

Many of the ideas would strike the outsider as silly or worse. For instance, in health services areas, there is great interest in the problem of back injuries among nursing staff. It's not necessarily the thing that comes first to mind when we think about the health care field. But if you reflect on it for a minute longer, it should be obvious that nurses and nursing staff do an awful lot of lifting in performing their jobs. They lift and push heavy equipment, and they lift and push oftentimes heavy patients! If 5 or 10 out of every hundred nursing staff were to strain their backs on average over the period of one year, the costs would be enormous—and that's pretty much what's happening. Even minor injuries can result in increased absenteeism. Major ones can result in lost jobs and expensive medical bills.

The nursing industry figures that this is a problem that costs tens of millions of dollars annually in increased health care. And, the health care industry has developed a number of approaches, many of them educational, to try to reduce the scope and cost of the problem. So, even though it might seem silly at first, many of these practical problems that arise in practice can lead to extensive research efforts.

Another source for research ideas is the literature in your specific field. Certainly, many researchers get ideas for research by reading the literature and thinking of ways to extend or refine previous research. Another type of literature that acts as a source of good research ideas is the Requests For Proposals (RFPs) that are published by government agencies and some companies.

These RFPs describe some problem that the agency would like researchers to address—they are virtually handing the researcher an idea! Typically, the RFP describes the problem that needs addressing, the contexts in which it operates, the approach they would like you to take to investigate to address the problem, and the amount they would be willing to pay for such research. Clearly, there's nothing like potential research funding to get researchers to focus on a particular research topic. And let's not forget the fact that many researchers simply think up their research topic on their own. Of course, no one lives in a vacuum, so we would expect that the ideas you come up with on your own are influenced by your background, culture, education and experiences.

There are several major considerations that come into play. Many of these involve making tradeoffs between rigor and practicality. To do a study well from a scientific point of view may force you to do things you wouldn't do normally. You may have to control the implementation of your programme more carefully than you otherwise might. Or, you may have to ask programme participants lots of questions that you usually wouldn't if you weren't doing research. If you had unlimited resources and unbridled control over the circumstances, you would always be able to do the best quality research. But those ideal circumstances seldom exist, and researchers are almost always forced to look for the best tradeoffs they can find in order to get the rigor they desire.

There are several practical considerations that almost always need to be considered when deciding on the feasibility of a research project. First, you have to think about how long the research will take to accomplish. Second, you have to question whether there are important ethical constraints that need consideration. Third, can you achieve the needed cooperation to take the project to its successful conclusion. And fourth, how significant are the costs of conducting the research. Failure to consider any of these factors can mean disaster later.

Concept Mapping Method

Social scientists have developed a number of methods and processes that might be useful in helping you to formulate a research project. This would include among these at least the following—brainstorming, brainwriting, nominal group techniques, focus groups, affinity mapping, Delphi techniques, facet theory, and qualitative text analysis. Concept mapping is a general method that can be used to help any individual or group to describe their ideas about some topic in a pictorial form. There are several different types of methods that all currently go by names like "concept mapping", "mental mapping" or "concept webbing."

All of them are similar in that they result in a picture of someone's ideas. But the kind of concept mapping describe here is different in a number of important ways.

— First, it is primarily a group process and so it is especially well-suited for situations where teams or groups of stakeholders have to work together. The other methods work primarily with individuals.

— Second, it uses a very structured facilitated approach. There are specific steps that are followed by a trained facilitator in helping a group to articulate its ideas and understand them more clearly.

— Third, the core of concept mapping consists of several state-of-the-art multivariate statistical methods that analyse the input from all of the individuals and yields an aggregate group product.

— And fourth, the method requires the use of specialised computer programmes that can handle the data from this type of process and accomplish the correct analysis and mapping procedures.

Although concept mapping is a general method, it is particularly useful for helping social researchers and research teams develop and detail ideas for research. And, it is especially valuable when researchers want to involve relevant stakeholder groups in the act of creating the research project. Although concept mapping is used for many purposes—strategic planning, product development, market analysis, decision making, measurement development—we concentrate here on it's potential for helping researchers formulate their projects.

So what is concept mapping? Essentially, concept mapping is a structured process, focused on a topic or construct of interest, involving input from one or more participants, that produces an interpretable pictorial view (concept map) of their ideas and concepts and how these are interrelated. Concept mapping helps people to think more effectively as a group without losing their individuality. It helps groups to manage the complexity of their ideas without trivialising them or losing detail.

A concept mapping process involves six steps that can take place in a single day or can be spread out over weeks or months depending on the situation.

- The first step is the Preparation Step. There are three things done here. The facilitator of the mapping process works with the initiator(s) (i.e., whoever requests the process initially) to identify who the participants will be. A mapping process can have hundreds or even thousands of stakeholders participating, although we usually have a relatively small group of between 10 and 20 stakeholders involved.
- Second, the initiator works with the stakeholders to develop the focus for the project. For instance, the group might decide to focus on defining a programme or treatment. Or, they might choose to

map all of the outcomes they might expect to see as a result.

- Finally, the group decides on an appropriate schedule for the mapping.

In the Generation Step the stakeholders develop a large set of statements that address the focus. For instance, they might generate statements that describe all of the specific activities that will constitute a specific social programme. Or, they might generate statements describing specific outcomes that might occur as a result of participating in a programme. A wide variety of methods can be used to accomplish this including traditional brainstorming, brainwriting, nominal group techniques, focus groups, qualitative text analysis, and so on. The group can generate up to 200 statements in a concept mapping project.

In the Structuring Step the participants do two things. First, each participant sorts the statements into piles of similar ones. Most times they do this by sorting a deck of cards that has one statement on each card. But they can also do this directly on a computer by dragging the statements into piles that they create. They can have as few or as many piles as they want. Each participant names each pile with a short descriptive label. Second, each participant rates each of the statements on some scale. Usually the statements are rated on a 1-to-5 scale for their relative importance, where a 1 means the statement is relatively unimportant compared to all the rest, a 3 means that it is moderately important, and a 5 means that it is extremely important.

The Representation Step is where the analysis is done—this is the process of taking the sort and rating input and "representing" it in map form. There are two major statistical analyses that are used.

The first—multidimensional scaling—takes the sort data across all participants and develops the basic map where each statement is a point on the map and statements that were piled together by more people are closer to each other on the map. The second analysis—cluster analysis—takes the output of the multidimensional scaling (the point map) and partitions the map into groups of statements or ideas, into clusters. If the statements describe activities of a programme, the clusters show how these can be grouped into logical groups of activities. If the statements are specific outcomes, the clusters might be viewed as outcome constructs or concepts. In the fifth step—the Interpretation Step—the facilitator works with the stakeholder group to help them develop their own labels and interpretations for the various maps.

Finally, the Utilisation Step involves using the maps to help address the original focus. On the programme side, the maps can be used as a visual framework for operationalising the programme. on the outcome side, they can be used as the basis for developing measures and displaying results.

3

Formulation of Social Work Research

As replacement strategies for capital accumulation have taken flight to locations unrestrained by the social and political commitments of industrial capitalism, the modern city in many respects seems to have become its own graveyard. The ruins and detritus of this once glorious engine of production span the contemporary cityscape as the discarded motifs and structures of a bygone era, recognisable in the myriad forms of urban blight that are perhaps most visible in the form of property abandonment.

Victim to the structural violence of uneven development, deindustrialisation, and suburbanisation, the modern city now stands as a debased and anaemic capillary system through which globalisation pulses in all of its forms. Philadelphia, oft described as the quintessential post-industrial rust belt city, has been especially hard hit in this regard. The visible fallout from these forces is evident in the erosion and abandonment of the built environment, with current estimates standing at 26,115 abandoned houses, 30,729 vacant lots, and 2,950 vacant commercial structures within city limits.

Other cities are facing similar problems in their urban cores but Philadelphia is said to have the worst problem with property abandonment—even worse than Detroit, the city most often associated with the woes of rust-belt decline. In fact, a recent Brookings Institute survey of 83 cities found that Philadelphia had the highest number of abandoned structures per capita in the country at a rate of 36.5 abandoned structures per 1000 residents. In recognition of the widespread postindustrial urban decline reflected in these numbers, Philadelphia Mayor John F. Street is currently staking his 25-year political career on a citywide "anti-blight" campaign in hopes of revitalising the city.

Street's self-proclaimed "war on blight," or "Neighbourhood Transformation Initiative" as it is known in formal terms, was signed into existence on March 14th, 2002. The anti-blight bill is a $295 million dollar bond initiative that is expected to induce an additional 1.4 billion dollars in state, federal and private spending over the next five years. Street's plan has been dubbed the "biggest political gamble of his career," and the media expects that it will provoke "nothing less than a citywide revolution". Discussions of urban blight in Street's political discourse are typically replete with references to the usual suspects: abandoned houses, abandoned factories, vacant lots, abandoned cars, graffiti, dirt, crime, rats, tires, garbage, illegal dumping, and other general signs of urban decay.

As part of a tightly synthesised and highly effective political rhetoric, Street's discussions of blight generally extend to the expansive rubric of its correlative problems, such as crime, disorder, drug dealing, poverty, declining tax bases and depressed land values, white flight, disinvestment, poor schools and community breakdown—all processes that are said to deteriorate quality of life in the city. Undoubtedly, the issue of urban blight weighs heavily upon the conscience of Philadelphia, thus making it a compelling topic for academic research. But the issue of how to make sense of "urban blight," or urban decline, is indeed a deeply complex matter that holds many risks and challenges.

The major theoretical paradigms seeking to explain urban blight offer myriad insights into the problems associated with urban blight, and each body of theory has advanced the knowledge base on blighted spaces in incrementally significant ways. Each of these theories is also limited in important and specific ways, particularly in terms of their restrictions on what can be known about the people living in blighted neighborhoods.

Spatially informed ethnography offers an opportunity to re-tell the story of urban blight in such a way that foregrounds the agency of the residents living in blighted neighborhoods—a factor that is conspicuously absent in conventional research, policy discourse, and media coverage. There are many ways of knowing, ethnography is an especially cogent framework for an alternative exploration of urban blight based on its appreciation for the immanently human configurations that play out in "blighted" neighborhoods.

Ethnographic research is valuable as it allows us to grasp the intertwined dynamics of cultural and material processes as they are played out in particular geographic locations, thus generating new forms of knowledge that elude the heuristics of conventional research methods. Recent transformations in urban anthropology suggest new ways to study the built environment through the integration of a broad array of spatial theoretical perspectives from cultural geography, political economy, urban sociology, and regional and city planning. The new emphasis on spatial relations provides insight into material, ideological and experiential aspects of the urban environment, while the reliance on ethnography allows researchers to present an experience-near account of the politics of everyday life in urban neighborhoods.

Simultaneously, this work addresses macro processes such as globalisation, commodification and the new urban social order in the context of local environments. Spatially informed urban ethnography incorporates critical interdisciplinary approaches en route to advancing the understanding of the city, thus providing geographical insights that are integral to the knowledge of the growing inequality of urban lives.

The proposed research is informed by these nascent academic trends, seeking to introduce new understandings of the specific issue of urban blight by introducing the following preliminary questions: What would it mean to focus on the ways in which human agency, imagination, and subjectivity are shaped by blighted geographical locations? What would it mean to pay ethnographic attention to how subjects in given historical conditions are shaped by blighted spaces, as well as how they respond to these spaces in culturally specific ways?

In advancing a new way to conceptualise urban blight, it is the primary objective of the proposed research to uphold the primacy of space and spatial theory not only in relation to questions of blighted environs, but also in relation to questions concerning the politics of everyday life. The questions raised by Henri Lefebvre's realisation that daily life depends on the production (and consumption) of space remain largely unanswered, even in academic works coming out of Marxist geography that hold the category of space as their primary raison d'etre.

As the built environment is critical to understanding the production and transformation of social relations, space is an important concept for social analysis. It is a multidimensional concept that is at once economic, political, semiotic and experiential, and in this sense it is an integral component of social interaction and an indispensable vector for critical theory, particularly when added to the vectors of time and being. The proposed research aspires to refrain from talking about space merely as an idealist or abstract category, in addition to avoiding simple discussions of space as strictly a container for the political economy.

Conversely, the proposed research will show how the consideration of socio-spatial relations can enhance the understanding of "blighted" urban environments by introducing an appreciation of culture in relation to material forces such as space, and by emphasizing the social relations that these material forces evoke. The primary objective will be to forge a relationship between the analytical categories of political economy, space, and culture through the lens of ethnography; as such the challenge will be to consider the reciprocal construction of culture within certain spatial locations, particularly in relation to processes of capital accumulation and politics.

As Michael Dear contends, "space is nature's way of preventing everything from happening in the same place". Henri Lefebvre staked much of his intellectual life on this simple proposition, yet the core of his work becomes infinitely more sophisticated when he draws the attention beyond mere inventories of what exists in space or a basic discourse on space—neither of which can produce a true knowledge of space. In contrast, Lefebvre's ontology asserts a greater importance for space as being present and implicit in the acts of creation and being, whereby the process of life itself is inextricably linked with the production of different spaces.

Contrary to the idea that space is merely a reified alembic that boxes things in, Lefebvre implores us to appreciate the built environment as being structured through social relationships. People create space; thus the production of space is an inherently political project in which space is a mediating force that integrates an infinite number of active and dynamic cultural processes. In appreciation of this premise, proponents of a revitalised cultural geography are seeking to advance the theoretical developments of cultural studies and social theory by informing these disciplines with a geographical sensibility.

Arguing that geography is not merely incidental to cultural variation nor relevant only to the explanation of diversity but rather fundamental to the very constitution of culture, Peter Jackson asserts the following: "If social processes do not take place on the head of a pin, then we need to take spatial structure seriously, not least in the production and communication of meaning that we call culture". Jackson's work insists that culture is a domain in which political, economic and social relations of domination and resistance are contested, negotiated and resolved. He further contends that culture is not merely socially constructed and geographically expressed but rather spatially constituted, thus it is vitally important to refrain from analysing these domains in isolation.

Such a conception lets on to an analysis of spatial manifestations of culture through a theoretically informed yet empirically grounded research methodology that places the relationship between culture, political economy, and space at centre stage. Yet much of the literature coming out of cultural geography remains highly abstract and theoretical.

The stakes of such a contribution become even more important when we consider the growing inequality of urban lives in the contemporary present. As Judith Goode & Jeff Maskovsky argue, we are facing a "new poverty" in the neoliberal era that has been shaped by the interconnecting phenomena of economic polarisation, political demobilisation, and market triumphalism. While these forces are not necessarily new in terms of the history of American poverty and politics, the extent to which each of these factors are mutually reinforcing one another en route to a wholesale dismantling of the liberal welfare state is virtually without historical precedent. Yet little is known about the conditions of poverty within the midst of these transitions, and as Goode & Maskovsky suggest, many of the cultural strategies taking shape are new and in urgent need of study.

The transition from a welfare state to a mode of spatial governmentality vis-à-vis a law and order state has created an influx of flexible, informal economic activities and post-welfare related "lifestyles." In recognition of these trends, this study proposes to offer a new and provocative way of looking at the various practices of daily life that are emerging in postindustrial neighborhoods. Exploring the lived realities of devolutionary measures, welfare reform, neo-conservative welfare retrenchment, and the withdrawal of city services will produce a picture of poverty informed by spatial theory which belies or at least displaces conventional representations.

Linking larger policy measures to the ground level of lived reality may elucidate such varied aspects as the regulation of the poor through policy; the engagement in strategies of underground economy as a viable mechanism to compensate for retrenchment and the macro-geographical shifts that have reshaped employment markets; and the act of carving out a coherent lifestyle through the utilisation of welfare programmes.

4

Research Design

Research design can be thought of as the structure of research—it is the "glue" that holds all of the elements in a research project together. A design using a concise notation that enables us to summarise a complex design structure efficiently. What are the "elements" that a design includes? They are:

Observations

These are symbolised by an 'O' in design notation. An O can refer to a single measure (e.g., a measure of body weight), a single instrument with multiple items (e.g., a 10-item self-esteem scale), a complex multi-part instrument (e.g., a survey), or a whole battery of tests or measures given out on one occasion. If you need to distinguish among specific measures, you can use subscripts with the O, as in O_1, O_2, and so on.

Treatments

These are symbolised with an 'X' in design notations. The X can refer to a simple intervention or to a complex hodgepodge programme (e.g., an employment training programme). Usually, a no-treatment control or comparison group has no symbol for the treatment. As with observations, you can use subscripts to distinguish different programmes or programme variations.

Groups

Each group in a design is given its own line in the design structure. If the design notation has three lines, there are three groups in the design.

Assignment to Group

Assignment to group is designated by a letter at the beginning of each line (i.e., group) that describes how the group was assigned. The major types of assignment are:

- R = random assignment
- N = nonequivalent groups
- C = assignment by cutoff
- Time

Time moves from left to right. Elements that are listed on the left occur before elements that are listed on the right.

Kinds of Designs

What are the different major types of research designs? We can classify designs into a simple threefold classification by asking some key questions. First, does the design use random assignment to groups? If random assignment is used, we call the design a randomised experiment or true experiment. If random assignment is not used, then we have to ask a second question: Does the design use either multiple groups or multiple waves of measurement? If the answer is yes, we would label it a quasi-experimental design. If no, we would call it a non-experimental design. This threefold classification is especially useful for describing the design with respect to internal validity. A randomised experiment generally is the strongest of the three designs when your interest is in establishing a cause-effect relationship.

A non-experiment is generally the weakest in this respect. In fact, the simplest form of non-experiment is a one-shot survey design that consists of nothing but a single observation O. This is probably one of the most common forms of research and, for some research questions—especially descriptive ones—is clearly a strong design. To illustrate the different types of designs, consider one of each in design notation.

- The first design is a post test-only randomised experiment. You can tell it's a randomised experiment because it has an R at the beginning of each line, indicating random assignment.
- The second design is a pre-post nonequivalent groups quasi-experiment. We know it's not a randomised experiment because random assignment wasn't used. And we know it's not a non-experiment because there are both multiple groups and multiple waves of measurement. That means it must be a quasi-experiment. We add the label "nonequivalent" because in this design we do not explicitly control the assignment and the groups may be nonequivalent or not similar to each other.
- Finally, we show a post test-only nonexperimental design. You might use this design if you want to study the effects of a natural disaster like a flood or tornado and you want to do so by interviewing survivors.

In this design, you don't have a comparison group and you don't have multiple waves of measurement. Does it make sense to do the non-experimental study? Of course! You could gain lots of valuable information by well-conducted post-disaster interviews. But you may have a hard time establishing which of the things you observed are due to the disaster rather than to other factors like the peculiarities of the town or pre-disaster characteristics.

Experimental Design

Experimental designs are often touted as the most "rigorous" of all research designs or, as the "gold standard" against which all other designs are judged. In one sense, they probably are. If you can implement an experimental design well, then the experiment is probably the strongest design with respect to internal validity. Why? Recall that internal validity is at the centre of all causal or cause-effect inferences. When you want to determine whether some programme or treatment causes some outcome or outcomes to occur, then you are interested in having strong internal validity. Essentially, you want to assess the proposition:

If X, then Y

or, in more colloquial terms:

If the programme is given, then the outcome occurs

Unfortunately, it's not enough just to show that when the programme or treatment occurs the expected outcome also happens. That's because there may be lots of reasons, other than the programme, for why you observed the outcome. To really show that there is a causal relationship, you have to simultaneously address the two propositions:

If X, then Y

and

If not X, then not Y

Or, once again more colloquially:

If the programme is given, then the outcome occurs

and

If the programme is not given, then the outcome does not occur

If you are able to provide evidence for both of these propositions, then you've in effect isolated the programme from all of the other potential causes of the outcome. You've shown that when the programme is present the outcome occurs and when it's not present, the outcome doesn't occur. That points to the causal effectiveness of the programme. Think of all this like a fork in the road. Down one path, you implement the programme and observe the outcome.

Down the other path, you don't implement the programme and the outcome doesn't occur. But, how do we take both paths in the road in the same study?. How can we be in two places at once? Ideally, what we want is to have the same conditions—the same people, context, time, and so on—and see whether when the programme is given we get the outcome and when the programme is not given we don't. Obviously, we can never achieve this hypothetical situation. If we give the programme to a group of people, we can't simultaneously not give it! So, how do we get out of this apparent dilemma?

Perhaps we just need to think about the problem a little differently. What if we could create two groups or contexts that are as similar as we can possibly make them? If we could be confident that the two situations are comparable, then we could administer our programme in one and not give the programme in the other. And, if the two contexts are comparable, then this is like taking both forks in the road simultaneously! We can have our cake and eat it too, so to speak. That's exactly what an experimental design tries to achieve.

In the simplest type of experiment, we create two groups that are "equivalent" to each other. One group gets the programme and the other group (the comparison or control group) does not. In all other respects, the groups are treated the same. They have similar people, live in similar contexts, have similar backgrounds, and so on. Now, if we observe differences in outcomes between these two groups, then the differences must be due to the only thing that differs between them—that one got the programme and the other didn't.

OK, so how do we create two groups that are "equivalent"? The approach used in experimental design is to assign people randomly from a common pool of people into the two groups. The experiment relies on this idea of random assignment to groups as the basis for obtaining two groups that are similar.

Then, we give one the programme or treatment and we don't give it to the other. We observe the same outcomes in both groups. The key to the success of the experiment is in the random assignment. In fact, even with random assignment we never expect that the groups we create will be exactly the same. How could they be, when they are made up of different people?

We rely on the idea of probability and assume that the two groups are "probabilistically equivalent" or equivalent within known probabilistic ranges. So, if we randomly assign people to two groups, and we have enough people in our study to achieve the desired probabilistic equivalence, then we may consider the experiment to be strong in internal validity and we probably have a good shot at assessing whether the programme causes the outcomes.

But there are lots of things that can go wrong. We may not have a large enough sample. Or, we may have people who refuse to participate in our study or who drop out part way through. Or, we may be challenged successfully on ethical grounds. Or, we may get resistance from the staff in our study who would like some of their "favourite" people to get the programme. Or, they mayor might insist that her daughter be put into the new programme in an educational study because it may mean she'll get better grades.

The bottom line here is that experimental design is intrusive and difficult to carry out in most real world contexts. And, because an experiment is often an intrusion, you are to some extent setting up an artificial situation so that you can assess your causal relationship with high internal validity. If so, then you are limiting the degree to which you can generalise your results to real contexts where you haven't set up an experiment. That is, you have reduced your external validity in order to achieve greater internal validity.

In the end, there is just no simple answer (no matter what anyone tells you!). If the situation is right, an experiment can be a very strong design to use. But it isn't automatically so. My own personal guess is that randomised experiments are probably appropriate in no more than 10% of the social research studies that attempt to assess causal relationships. Experimental design is a fairly complex subject in its own right.

Two-Group Experimental Designs

The simplest of all experimental designs is the two-group post test-only randomised experiment. In design notation, it has two lines—one for each group—with an R at the beginning of each line to indicate that the groups were randomly assigned. One group gets the treatment or programme (the X) and the other group is the comparison group and doesn't get the programme. Notice that a pretest is not required for this design. Usually we include a pretest in order to determine whether groups are comparable prior to the programme, but because we are using random assignment we can assume that the two groups are probabilistically equivalent to begin with and the pretest is not required.

In this design, we are most interested in determining whether the two groups are different after the programme. Typically we measure the groups on one or more measures (the Os in notation) and we compare them by testing for the differences between the means using a t-test or one way Analysis of Variance (ANOVA). The post test-only randomised experiment is strong against the single-group threats to internal validity because it's not a single group design! (Tricky, huh?) It's strong against the all of the multiple-group threats except for selection-mortality. For instance, it's strong against selection-testing and selection-instrumentation because it doesn't use repeated measurement.

The selection-mortality threat is especially salient if there are differential rates of dropouts in the two groups. This could result if the treatment or programme is a noxious or negative one (e.g., a painful medical procedure like chemotherapy) or if the control group condition is painful or intolerable. This design is susceptible to all of the social interaction threats to internal validity.

Because the design requires random assignment, in some institutional settings (e.g., schools) it is more likely to utilise persons who would be aware of each other and of the conditions they've been assigned to. The post test-only randomised experimental design is, despite its simple structure, one of the best research designs for assessing cause-effect relationships. It is easy to execute and, because it uses only a post test, is relatively inexpensive. But there are many variations on this simple experimental design. You can begin to explore these by looking at how we classify the various experimental designs.

Probabilistic Equivalence

Two groups are equal to each other. When we deal with human beings it is impossible to ever say that any two individuals or groups are equal or equivalent. Clearly the important term in the phrase is "probabilistic". This means that the type of equivalence we have is based on the notion of probabilities.

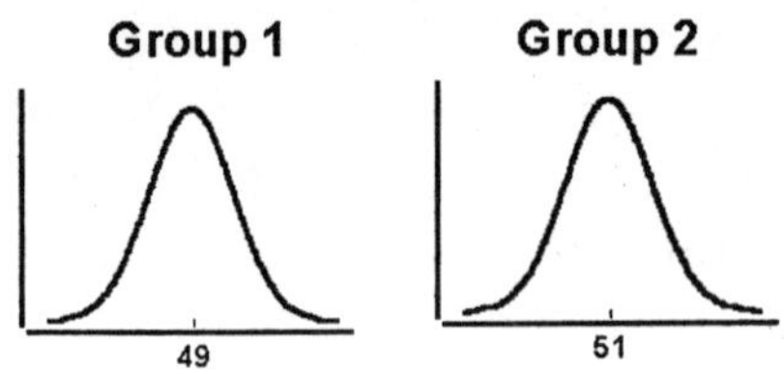

With α = .05, we expect that we will observe a pretest difference 5 times out of 100

In more concrete terms, probabilistic equivalence means that we know perfectly the odds that we will find a difference between two groups. Notice, it doesn't mean that the means of the two groups will be equal. It just means that we know the odds that they won't be equal. The figure shows two groups, one having a mean of 49 and the other with a mean of 51. Could these two groups be probabilistically equivalent? Certainly!

We achieve probabilistic equivalence through the mechanism of random assignment to groups. When we randomly assign to groups, we can calculate the chance that the two groups will differ just because of the random assignment (i.e., by chance alone). Let's say we are assigning a group of first grade students to two groups. Further, let's assume that the average test scores for these children for a standardised test with a population mean of 50 were 49 and 51 respectively.

We might conduct a t-test to see if the means of our two randomly assigned groups are statistically different. We know—through random assignment and the law of large numbers—that the chance that they will be different is 5 out of 100 when we set our significance level to.05 (i.e., alpha =.05). In other words, 5 times out of every 100, when we randomly assign two groups, we can expect to get a significant difference at the. 05 level of significance.

When we assign randomly, the only reason the groups can differ is because of chance assignment because their assignment is entirely based on the randomness of assignment. If, by chance, the groups differ on one variable, we have no reason to believe that they will automatically be different on any other. Even if we find that the groups differ on a pretest, we have no reason to suspect that they will differ on a posttest. Why? Because their pretest difference had to be a chance one. So, when we randomly assign, we are able to assume that the groups do have a form of equivalence. We don't expect them to be equal. But we do expect that they are "probabilistically" equal.

Random Selection and Assignment

Random selection is how you draw the sample of people for your study from a population. Random assignment is how you assign the sample that you draw to different groups or treatments in your study. It is possible to have both random selection and assignment in a study. Let's say you drew a random sample of 100 clients from a population list of 1000 current clients of your organisation. That is random sampling. Now, let's say you randomly assign 50 of these clients to get some new additional treatment and the other 50 to be controls. That's random assignment.

It is also possible to have only one of these (random selection or random assignment) but not the other in a study. For instance, if you do not randomly draw the 100 cases from your list of 1000 but instead just take the first

100 on the list, you do not have random selection. But you could still randomly assign this nonrandom sample to treatment versus control. Or, you could randomly select 100 from your list of 1000 and then nonrandomly (haphazardly) assign them to treatment or control. And, it's possible to have neither random selection nor random assignment. In a typical nonequivalent groups design in education you might nonrandomly choose two 5th grade classes to be in your study. This is nonrandom selection. Then, you could arbitrarily assign one to get the new educational programme and the other to be the control. This is nonrandom (or nonequivalent) assignment.

Random selection is related to sampling. Therefore it is most related to the external validity (or generalisability) of your results. After all, we would randomly sample so that our research participants better represent the larger group from which they're drawn. Random assignment is most related to design. In fact, when we randomly assign participants to treatments we have, by definition, an experimental design. Therefore, random assignment is most related to internal validity. After all, we randomly assign in order to help assure that our treatment groups are similar to each other (i.e., equivalent) prior to the treatment.

Effect of Randomised Block Designs

The Randomised Block Design is research design's equivalent to stratified random sampling. Like stratified sampling, randomised block designs are constructed to reduce noise or variance in the data. How do they do it? They require that the researcher divide the sample into relatively homogeneous subgroups or blocks. Then, the experimental design you want to implement is implemented within each block or homogeneous subgroup. The key idea is that the variability within each block is less than the variability of the entire sample.

Thus each estimate of the treatment effect within a block is more efficient than estimates across the entire sample. And, when we pool these more efficient estimates across blocks, we should get an overall more efficient estimate than we would without blocking.

Covariance Designs

The basic Analysis of Covariance Design (ANCOVA or ANACOVA) is a just pretest-posttest randomised experimental design. The notation shown here suggests that the pre-programme measure is the same one as the post-programme measure, and so we would call this a pretest. But you should note that the pre-programme measure doesn't have to be a pretest—it can be any variable measured prior to the programme intervention. It is also possible for a study to have more than one covariate.

The pre-programme measure or pretest is sometimes also called a "covariate" because of the way it's used in the data analysis—we "covary" it with the outcome variable or posttest in order to remove variability or noise. Thus, the ANCOVA design falls in the class of a "noise reduction" experimental design. In social research we frequently hear about statistical "adjustments" that attempt to control for important factors in our study. For instance, we might read that an analysis "examined posttest performance after adjusting for the income and educational level of the participants." In this case, "income" and "education level" are covariates.

Covariates are the variables you "adjust for" in your study. Sometimes the language that will be used is that of "removing the effects" of one variable from another. For instance, we might read that an analysis "examined posttest performance after removing the effect of income and educational level of the participants."

Hybrid Experimental Designs

Hybrid experimental designs are just what the name implies—new strains that are formed by combining features of more established designs. There are lots of variations that could be constructed from standard design features.

Solomon Four-Group Design

The Solomon Four-Group Design is designed to deal with a potential testing threat. Recall that a testing threat occurs when the act of taking a test affects how people score on a retest or posttest. It's probably not a big surprise that this design has four groups. Note that two of the groups receive the treatment and two do not. Further, two of the groups receive a pretest and two do not. One way to view this is as a 2x2 (Treatment Group X Measurement Group) factorial design. Within each treatment condition we have a group that is pretested and one that is not. By explicitly including testing as a factor in the design, we are able to assess experimentally whether a testing threat is operating.

Possible Outcomes. Let's look at a couple of possible outcomes from this design. The first outcome graph shows what the data might look like if there is a treatment or programme effect and there is no testing threat. You need to be careful in interpreting this graph to note that there are six dots—one to represent the average for each O in the design notation. To help you visually see the connection between the pretest and posttest average for the same group, a line is used to connect the dots. The two dots that are not connected by a line represent the two post-only groups. Look first at the two pretest means. They are close to each because the groups were randomly assigned. On the posttest, both treatment groups outscored both controls.

Now, look at the posttest values. There appears to be no difference between the treatment groups, even though one got a pretest and the other did not. Similarly, the two control groups scored about the same on the posttest. Thus, the pretest did not appear to affect the outcome. But both treatment groups clearly outscored both controls. There is a main effect for the treatment.

Now, look at a result where there is evidence of a testing threat. In this outcome, the pretests are again equivalent (because the groups were randomly assigned). Each treatment group outscored it's comparable control group. The pre-post treatment outscored the pre-post control. And, the post-only treatment outscored the post-only control. These results indicate that there is a treatment effect. But here, both groups that had the pretest outscored their comparable non-pretest group. That's evidence for a testing threat.

Switching Replications Design

The Switching Replications design is one of the strongest of the experimental designs. And, when the circumstances are right for this design, it addresses one of the major problems in experimental designs—the need to deny the programme to some participants through random assignment.

The design notation indicates that this is a two group design with three waves of measurement. You might think of this as two pre-post treatment-control designs grafted together. That is, the implementation of the treatment is repeated or replicated. And in the repetition of the treatment, the two groups switch roles—the original control group becomes the treatment group in phase 2 while the original treatment acts as the control. By the end of the study all participants have received the treatment.

The switching replications design is most feasible in organisational contexts where programmes are repeated at regular intervals. For instance, it works especially well in schools that are on a semester system. All students are pretested at the beginning of the school year. During the first semester, Group 1 receives the treatment and during the second semester Group 2 gets it. The design also enhances organisational efficiency in resource allocation. Schools only need to allocate enough resources to give the programme to half of the students at a time.

Possible Outcomes. Let's look at two possible outcomes. In the first example, we see that when the programme is given to the first group, the recipients do better than the controls. In the second phase, when the programme is given to the original controls, they "catch up" to the original programme group. Thus, we have a converge, diverge, reconverge outcome pattern. We might expect a result like this when the programme covers specific content that the students master in the short term and where we don't expect that they will continue getting better as a result.

Now, look at the other example result. During the first phase we see the same result as before—the programme group improves while the control does not. And, as before, during the second phase we see the original control group, now the programme group, improve as much as did the first programme group. But now, during phase two, the original programme group continues to increase even though the programme is no longer being given them. Why would this happen? It could happen in circumstances where the programme has continuing and longer term effects. For instance, if the programme focused on learning skills, students might continue to improve even after the formal programme period because they continue to apply the skills and improve in them.

Internal Validity

Internal Validity is the approximate truth about inferences regarding cause-effect or causal relationships. Thus, internal validity is only relevant in studies that try to establish a causal relationship. It's not relevant in most observational or descriptive studies, for instance. But for studies that assess the effects of social programmes or interventions, internal validity is perhaps the primary consideration.

In those contexts, you would like to be able to conclude that your programme or treatment made a difference—it improved test scores or reduced symptomology. But there may be lots of reasons, other than your programme, why test scores may improve or symptoms may reduce. The key question in internal validity is whether observed changes can be attributed to your programme or intervention and not to other possible causes.

One of the things that's most difficult to grasp about internal validity is that it is only relevant to the specific study in question. That is, you can think of internal validity as a "zero generalisability" concern. All that internal validity means is that you have evidence that what you did in the study caused what you observed to happen. It doesn't tell you whether what you did for the programme was what you wanted to do or whether what you observed was what you wanted to observe—those are construct validity concerns. It is possible to have internal validity in a study and not have construct validity. For instance, imagine a study where you are looking at the effects of a new computerised tutoring programme on math performance in first grade students.

Imagine that the tutoring is unique in that it has a heavy computer game component and you think that's what will really work to improve math performance.

Finally, imagine that you were wrong—it turns out that math performance did improve, and that it was because of something you did, but that it had nothing to do with the computer programme. What caused the improvement was the individual attention that the adult tutor gave to the child—the computer programme didn't make any difference.

This study would have internal validity because something that you did affected something that you observed—you did cause something to happen. But the study would not have construct validity, specifically, the label "computer math programme" does not accurately describe the actual cause. Since the key issue in internal validity is the causal one, we'll begin by considering what conditions need to be met in order to establish a causal relationship in your project. Then we'll consider the different threats to internal validity—the kinds of criticisms your critics will raise when you try to conclude that your programme caused the outcome.

Establishing Cause and Effect

Cause-Effect Relationship

How do we establish a cause-effect (causal) relationship? What criteria do we have to meet? Generally, there are three criteria that you must meet before you can say that you have evidence for a causal relationship:

Temporal precedence

First, you have to be able to show that your cause happened before your effect. Sounds easy, huh? Of course my cause has to happen before the effect. Did you ever hear of an effect happening before its cause? Before we get lost in the logic here, consider a classic example from economics: does inflation cause unemployment? It certainly seems plausible that as inflation increases, more employers find that in order to meet costs they have to lay off employees.

So it seems that inflation could, at least partially, be a cause for unemployment. But both inflation and employment rates are occurring together on an ongoing basis. Is it possible that fluctuations in employment can affect inflation? If we have an increase in the work force (i.e., lower unemployment) we may have more demand for goods, which would tend to drive up the prices (i.e., inflate them) at least until supply can catch up. So which is the cause and which the effect, inflation or unemployment? It turns out that in this kind of cyclical situation involving ongoing processes that interact that both may cause and, in turn, be affected by the other. This makes it very hard to establish a causal relationship in this situation.

Covariation of the cause and effect

What does this mean? Before you can show that you have a causal relationship you have to show that you have some type of relationship. For instance, consider the syllogism:

if X then Y

if not X then not Y

If you observe that whenever X is present, Y is also present, and whenever X is absent, Y is too, then you have demonstrated that there is a relationship between X and Y. Let's put this same syllogism in programme evaluation terms:

if programme then outcome

if not programme then not outcome

Or, in colloquial terms: if you give a programme you observe the outcome but if you don't give the programme you don't observe the outcome. This provides evidence that the programme and outcome are related.

Notice, however, that this syllogism doesn't not provide evidence that the programme caused the outcome—perhaps there was some other factor present with the programme that caused the outcome, rather than the programme. The relationships described so far are rather simple binary relationships. Sometimes we want to know whether different amounts of the programme lead to different amounts of the outcome—a continuous relationship:

if more of the programme then more of the outcome

if less of the programme then less of the outcome

Just because you show there's a relationship doesn't mean it's a causal one. It's possible that there is some other variable or factor that is causing the outcome. This is sometimes referred to as the "third variable" or "missing variable" problem and it's at the heart of the issue of internal validity. What are some of the possible plausible alternative explanations? Just go look at the threats to internal validity—each one describes a type of alternative explanation.

In order for you to argue that you have demonstrated internal validity—that you have shown there's a causal relationship—you have to "rule out" the plausible alternative explanations. How do you do that? One of the major ways is with your research design. Let's consider a simple single group threat to internal validity, a history threat.

Let's assume you measure your programme group before they start the programme (to establish a baseline), you give them the programme, and then you measure their performance afterwards in a posttest. You see a marked improvement in their performance which you would like to infer is caused by your programme.

One of the plausible alternative explanations is that you have a history threat—it's not your programme that caused the gain but some other specific historical event. For instance, it's not your anti-smoking campaign that caused the reduction in smoking but rather the Surgeon General's latest report that happened to be issued between the time you gave your pretest and posttest. How do you rule this out with your research design?

One of the simplest ways would be to incorporate the use of a control group—a group that is comparable to your programme group with the only difference being that they didn't receive the programme.

But they did experience the Surgeon General's latest report. If you find that they didn't show a reduction in smoking even though they did experience the same Surgeon General report you have effectively "ruled out" the Surgeon General's report as a plausible alternative explanation for why you observed the smoking reduction.

In most applied social research that involves evaluating programmes, temporal precedence is not a difficult criterion to meet because you administer the programme before you measure effects.

And, establishing covariation is relatively simple because you have some control over the programme and can set things up so that you have some people who get it and some who don't (if X and if not X). Typically the most difficult criterion to meet is the third—ruling out alternative explanations for the observed effect. That is why research design is such an important issue and why it is intimately linked to the idea of internal validity.

Single Group Threats

Single Group Case

What is meant by a "single group" threat? Let's consider

two single group designs and then consider the threats that are most relevant with respect to internal validity. The top design in the figure shows a "posttest-only" single group design.

Here, a group of people receives your programme and afterwards is given a posttest. In the bottom part of the figure we see a "pretest-posttest" single group design. In this case, we give the participants a pretest or baseline measure, give them the programme or treatment, and then give them a posttest.

To help make this a bit more concrete, let's imagine that we are studying the effects of a compensatory education programme in mathematics for first grade students on a measure of math performance such as a standardized math achievement test. In the post-only design, we would give the first graders the programme and then give a math achievement posttest.

We might choose not to give them a baseline measure because we have reason to believe they have no prior knowledge of the math skills we are teaching. It wouldn't make sense to pretest them if we expect they would all get a score of zero.

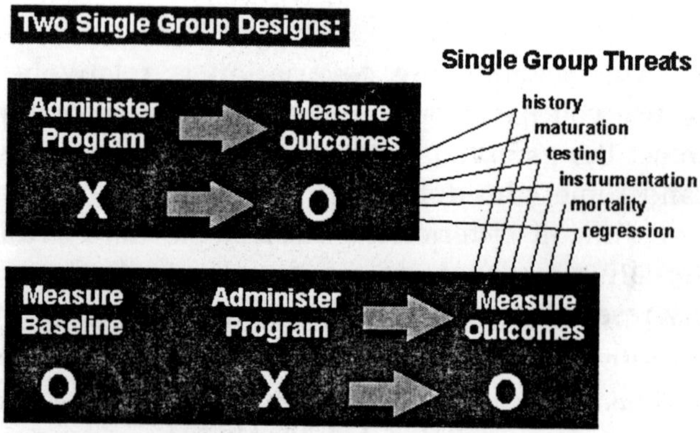

In the pre-post design we are not willing to assume that they have no prior knowledge. We measure the baseline in order to determine where the students start out in math achievement. We might hypothesize that the change or gain from pretest to posttest is due to our special math tutoring programme. This is a compensatory programme because it is only given to students who are identified as potentially low in math ability on the basis of some screening mechanism.

Single Group Threats

With either of these scenarios in mind, consider what would happen if you observe a certain level of posttest math achievement or a change or gain from pretest to posttest. You want to conclude that the outcome is due to your math programme. How could you be wrong? Here are some of the ways, some of the threats to interval validity that your critics might raise, some of the plausible alternative explanations for your observed effect:

History threat

It's not your math programme that caused the outcome, it's something else, some historical event that occurred. For instance, we know that lot's of first graders watch the public TV programme Sesame Street. And, we know that in every Sesame Street show they present some very elementary math concepts. Perhaps these shows cause the outcome and not your math programme.

Maturation threat

The children would have had the exact same outcome even if they had never had your special math training programme. All you are doing is measuring normal maturation or growth in understanding that occurs as part of growing up—your math programme has no effect.

How is this maturation explanation different from a history threat? In general, if we're talking about a specific event or chain of events that could cause the outcome, we call it a history threat. If we're talking about all of the events that typically transpire in your life over a period of time we call it a maturation threat.

Testing threat

This threat only occurs in the pre-post design. What if taking the pretest made some of the children more aware of that kind of math problem—it "primed" them for the programme so that when you began the math training they were ready for it in a way that they wouldn't have been without the pretest. This is what is meant by a testing threat—taking the pretest affects how participants do on the posttest.

Instrumentation threat

Like the testing threat, this one only operates in the pretest-posttest situation. What if the change from pretest to posttest is due not to your math programme but rather to a change in the test that was used? This is what's meant by an instrumentation threat. In many schools when they have to administer repeated testing they don't use the exact same test (in part because they're worried about a testing threat!) but rather give out "alternate forms" of the same tests.

These alternate forms were designed to be "equivalent" in the types of questions and level of difficulty, but what if they aren't? Perhaps part or all of any pre-post gain is attributable to the change in instrument, not to your programme. Instrumentation threats are especially likely when the "instrument" is a human observer. The observers may get tired over time or bored with the observations. Conversely, they might get better at making the observations as they practice more. In either event, it's the change in instrumentation, not the programme, that leads to the outcome.

Mortality threat

Mortality doesn't mean that people in your study are dying. Mortality is used metaphorically here. It means that people are "dying" with respect to your study. Usually, it means that they are dropping out of the study. What's wrong with that? Let's assume that in our compensatory math tutoring programme we have a nontrivial dropout rate between pretest and posttest. And, assume that the kids who are dropping out are the low pretest math achievement test scorers.

If you look at the average gain from pretest to posttest using all of the scores available to you at each occasion, you would include these low pretest subsequent dropouts in the pretest and not in the posttest. You'd be dropping out the potential low scorers from the posttest, or, you'd be artificially inflating the posttest average over what it would have been if no students had dropped out. And, you won't necessarily solve this problem by comparing pre-post averages for only those kids who stayed in the study. This subsample would certainly not be representative even of the original entire sample.

Furthermore, we know that because of regression threats these students may appear to actually do worse on the posttest, simply as an artifact of the non-random dropout or mortality in your study. When mortality is a threat, the researcher can often gauge the degree of the threat by comparing the dropout group against the nondropout group on pretest measures. If there are no major differences, it may be more reasonable to assume that mortality was happening across the entire sample and is not biasing results greatly. But if the pretest differences are large, one must be concerned about the potential biasing effects of mortality.

Regression threat

A regression threat, also known as a "regression artifact" or "regression to the mean" is a statistical phenomenon that occurs whenever you have a nonrandom sample from a population and two measures that are imperfectly correlated. Let me try again. Assume that your two measures are a pretest and posttest. Furthermore, assume that your sample consists of low pretest scorers. The regression threat means that the pretest average for the group in your study will appear to increase or improve (relatively to the overall population) even if you don't do anything to them—even if you never give them a treatment.

Regression is a confusing threat to understand at first. It as the "you can only go up from here" phenomenon. If you include in your programme only the kids who constituted the lowest ten percent of the class on the pretest, what are the chances that they would constitute exactly the lowest ten percent on the posttest? Not likely. Most of them would score low on the posttest, but they aren't likely to be the lowest ten percent twice.

For instance, maybe there were a few kids on the pretest who got lucky on a few guesses and scored at the eleventh percentile who won't get so lucky next time. No, if you choose the lowest ten percent on the pretest, they can't get any lower than being the lowest—they can only go up from there, relative to the larger population from which they were selected. This purely statistical phenomenon is what we mean by a regression threat.

How do we deal with these single group threats to internal validity? While there are several ways to rule out threats, one of the most common approaches to ruling out the ones listed above is through your research design. For instance, instead of doing a single group study, you could incorporate a control group. In this scenario, you would have two groups: one receives your programme and the other one doesn't. In fact, the only difference between these groups should be the programme. If that's true, then the control group would experience all the same history and maturation threats, would have the same testing and instrumentation issues, and would have similar rates of mortality and regression to the mean.

In other words, a good control group is one of the most effective ways to rule out the single-group threats to internal validity. Of course, when you add a control group, you no-longer have a single group design. And, you will still have to deal with threats two major types of threats to internal validity: the multiple-group threats to internal validity and the social threats to internal validity.

Regression to the Mean

A regression threat, also known as a "regression artifact" or "regression to the mean" is a statistical phenomenon that occurs whenever you have a nonrandom sample from a population and two measures that are imperfectly correlated. The figure shows the regression to the mean phenomenon.

The top part of the figure shows the pretest distribution for a population. Pretest scores are "normally" distributed, the frequency distribution looks like a "bell-shaped" curve. Assume that the sample for your study was selected exclusively from the low pretest scorers. You can see on the top part of the figure where their pretest mean is—clearly, it is considerably below the population average. What would we predict the posttest to look like? First, let's assume that your programme or treatment doesn't work at all (the "null" case).

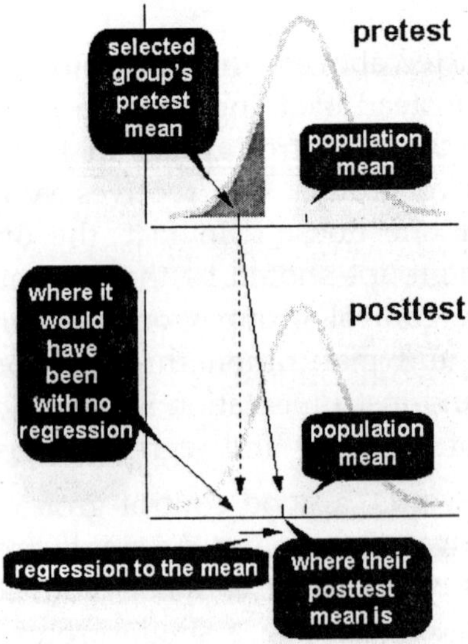

Our naive assumption would be that our sample would score just as badly on the posttest as they did on the pretest. But they don't! The bottom of the figure shows where the sample's posttest mean would have been without regression and where it actually is. In actuality, the sample's posttest mean wound up closer to the posttest population mean than their pretest mean was to the pretest population mean. In other words, the sample's mean appears to regress toward the mean of the population from pretest to posttest.

Let's start with a simple explanation and work from there. To see why regression to the mean happens, consider a concrete case. In your study you select the lowest 10% of the population based on their pretest score. What are the chances that on the posttest that exact group will once again constitute the lowest ten percent? Not likely. Most of them will probably be in the lowest ten percent on the posttest, but if even just a few are not, then their group's mean will have to be closer to the population's posttest than it was to the pretest.

The same thing is true on the other end. If you select as your sample the highest ten percent pretest scorers, they aren't likely to be the highest ten percent on the posttest (even though most of them may be in the top ten percent). If even just a few score below the top ten percent on the posttest their group's posttest mean will have to be closer to the population posttest mean than to their pretest mean. Here are a few things you need to know about the regression to the mean phenomenon:

Statistical phenomenon

Regression toward the mean occurs for two reasons. First, it results because you asymmetrically sampled from the population. If you randomly sample from the population, you would observe (subject to random error) that the population and your sample have the same pretest average. Because the sample is already at the population mean on the pretest, it is impossible for them to regress towards the mean of the population any more!

Goup phenomenon

You cannot tell which way an individual's score will move based on the regression to the mean phenomenon. Even though the group's average will move toward the population's, some individuals in the group are likely to move in the other direction.

Here's a common research mistake. You run a programme and don't find any overall group effect. So, you decide to look at those who did best on the posttest (your "success" stories!?) and see how much they gained over the pretest. You are selecting a group that is extremely high on the posttest. They won't likely all be the best on the pretest as well. So, their pretest mean has to be closer to the population mean than their posttest one. You describe this nice "gain" and are almost ready to write up your results when someone suggests you look at your "failure" cases, the people who score worst on your posttest. When you check on how they were doing on the pretest you find that they weren't the worst scorers there.

If they had been the worst scorers both times, you would have simply said that your programme didn't have any effect on them. But now it looks worse than that—it looks like your programme actually made them worse relative to the population! What will you do? How will you ever get your grant renewed? Or your paper published? Or, heaven help you, how will you ever get tenured?

Relative phenomenon

It has nothing to do with overall maturational trends. It could be that everyone in the population gains 20 points (on average) between the pretest and the posttest. But regression to the mean would still be operating, even in that case. That is, the low scorers would, on average, be gaining more than the population gain of 20 points.

If your sample consists of below-population-mean scorers, the regression to the mean will make it appear that they move up on the other measure. But if your sample consists of high scorers, their mean will appear to move down relative to the population.

If your sample differs from the population by only a little bit on the first measure, there won't be much regression to the mean because there isn't much room for them to regress—they're already near the population mean. So, if you have a sample, even a nonrandom one, that is a pretty good subsample of the population, regression to the mean will be inconsequential (although it will be present). But if your sample is very extreme relative to the population (e.g., the lowest or highest x%), their mean is further from the population's and has more room to regress.

The other major factor that affects the amount of regression to the mean is the correlation between the two variables. If the two variables are perfectly correlated—the highest scorer on one is the highest on the other, next highest on one is next highest on the other, and so on—there will no be regression to the mean. But this is unlikely to ever occur in practice. We know from measurement theory that there is no such thing as "perfect" measurement—all measurement is assumed to have some random error in measurement. It is only when the measure has no random error—is perfectly reliable—that we can expect it will be able to correlate perfectly. Since that just doesn't happen in the real world, we have to assume that measures have some degree of unreliability, and that relationships between measures will not be perfect, and that there will appear to be regression to the mean between these two measures, given asymmetrically sampled subgroups.

MULTIPLE GROUP THREATS

Central Issue

A multiple-group design typically involves at least two groups and before-after measurement. Most often, one group receives the programme or treatment while the other does not and constitutes the "control" or comparison group. But sometimes one group gets the programme and the other gets either the standard programme or another programme you would like to compare. In this case, you would be comparing two programmes for their relative outcomes. Typically you would construct a multiple-group design so that you could compare the groups directly.

In such designs, the key internal validity issue is the degree to which the groups are comparable before the study. If they are comparable, and the only difference between them is the programme, posttest differences can be attributed to the programme. But that's a big if. If the groups aren't comparable to begin with, you won't know how much of the outcome to attribute to your programme or to the initial differences between groups.

There really is only one multiple group threat to internal validity: that the groups were not comparable before the study. We call this threat a selection bias or selection threat. A selection threat is any factor other than the programme that leads to posttest differences between groups. Whenever we suspect that outcomes differ between groups not because of our programme but because of prior group differences we are suspecting a selection bias.

Although the term 'selection bias' is used as the general category for all prior differences, when we know specifically what the group difference is, we usually hyphenate it with the 'selection' term. The multiple-group selection threats directly parallel the single group threats. For instance, while we have 'history' as a single group threat, we have 'selection-history' as its multiple-group analogue.

As with the single group threats to internal validity, we'll assume a simple example involving a new compensatory mathematics tutoring programme for first graders. The design will be a pretest-posttest design, and we will divide the first graders into two groups, one getting the new tutoring programme and the other not getting it.

Here are the major multiple-group threats to internal validity for this case:

— *Selection-History Threat:* A selection-history threat is any other event that occurs between pretest and posttest that the groups experience differently. Because this is a selection threat, it means the groups differ in some way. Because it's a 'history' threat, it means that the way the groups differ is with respect to their reactions to history events. For example, what if the children in one group differ from those in the other in their television habits. Perhaps the programme group children watch Sesame Street more frequently than those in the control group do. Since Sesame Street is a children's show that presents simple mathematical concepts in interesting ways, it may be that a higher average posttest math score for the programme group doesn't indicate the effect of our math tutoring—it's really an effect of the two groups differentially experiencing a relevant event—in this case Sesame Street—between the pretest and posttest.

— *Selection-Maturation Threat:* A selection-maturation threat results from differential rates of normal growth between pretest and posttest for the groups. In this case, the two groups are different in their different rates of maturation with respect to math concepts. It's important to distinguish between history and maturation threats. In general, history refers to a discrete event or series of events whereas maturation implies the normal, ongoing developmental process that would take place. In any case, if the groups are maturing at different rates with respect to the outcome, we cannot assume that posttest differences are due to our programme—they may be selection-maturation effects.

— *Selection-Testing Threat:* A selection-testing threat occurs when there is a differential effect between groups on the posttest of taking the pretest. Perhaps the test "primed" the children in each group differently or they may have learned differentially from the pretest. in these cases, an observed posttest difference can't be attributed to the programme, they could be the result of selection-testing.

- *Selection-Instrumentation Threat:* Selection-instrumentation refers to any differential change in the test used for each group from pretest and posttest. In other words, the test changes differently for the two groups. Perhaps the test consists of observers who rate the class performance of the children. What if the programme group observers for example, get better at doing the observations while, over time, the comparison group observers get fatigued and bored. Differences on the posttest could easily be due to this differential instrumentation—selection-instrumentation—and not to the programme.
- *Selection-Mortality Threat:* Selection-mortality arises when there is differential nonrandom dropout between pretest and posttest. In our example, different types of children might drop out of each group, or more may drop out of one than the other. Posttest differences might then be due to the different types of dropouts—the selection-mortality—and not to the programme.
- *Selection-Regression Threat:* Finally, selection-regression occurs when there are different rates of regression to the mean in the two groups. This might happen if one group is more extreme on the pretest than the other. In the context of our example, it may be that the programme group is getting a disproportionate number of low math ability children because teachers think they need the math tutoring more (and the teachers don't understand the need for 'comparable' programme and comparison groups!). Since the tutoring group has the more extreme lower scorers, their mean will regress a greater distance toward the overall population mean and they will appear to gain more than their comparison group counterparts. This is

not a real programme gain—it's just a selection-regression artifact.

When we move from a single group to a multiple group study, what do we gain from the rather significant investment in a second group? If the second group is a control group and is comparable to the programme group, we can rule out the single group threats to internal validity because they will all be reflected in the comparison group and cannot explain why posttest group differences would occur. But the key is that the groups must be comparable. How can we possibly hope to create two groups that are truly "comparable"?

The only way we know of doing that is to randomly assign persons in our sample into the two groups—we conduct a randomised or "true" experiment. But in many applied research settings we can't randomly assign, either because of logistical or ethical factors. In that case, we typically try to assign two groups nonrandomly so that they are as equivalent as we can make them. We might, for instance, have one classroom of first graders assigned to the math tutoring programme while the other class is the comparison group. In this case, we would hope the two are equivalent, and we may even have reasons to believe that they are.

But because they may not be equivalent and because we did not use a procedure like random assignment to at least assure that they are probabilistically equivalent, we call such designs quasi-experimental designs. If we measure them on a pretest, we can examine whether they appear to be similar on key measures before the study begins and make some judgement about the plausibility that a selection bias exists. Even if we move to a multiple group design and have confidence that our groups are comparable, we cannot assume that we have strong internal validity. There are a number of social threats to internal validity that arise from the human interaction present in applied social research that we will also need to address.

Social Interaction Threats

Applied social research is a human activity. And, the results of such research are affected by the human interactions involved. The social threats to internal validity refer to the social pressures in the research context that can lead to posttest differences that are not directly caused by the treatment itself. Most of these threats occur because the various groups (e.g., programme and comparison), or key people involved in carrying out the research (e.g., managers and administrators, teachers and principals) are aware of each other's existence and of the role they play in the research project or are in contact with one another.

Many of these threats can be minimized by isolating the two groups from each other, but this leads to other problems. Here are the major social interaction threats to internal validity:

Imitation of treatment

This occurs when a comparison group learns about the programme either directly or indirectly from programme group participants. In a school context, children from different groups within the same school might share experiences during lunch hour. Or, comparison group students, seeing what the programme group is getting, might set up their own experience to try to imitate that of the programme group. In either case, if the diffusion of imitation affects the posttest performance of the comparison group, it can have an jeopardize your ability to assess whether your programme is causing the outcome. Notice that this threat to validity tend to equalise the outcomes between groups, minimizing the chance of seeing a programme effect even if there is one.

Compensatory rivalry

Here, the comparison group knows what the programme group is getting and develops a competitive attitude with them. The students in the comparison group might see the special math tutoring programme the programme group is getting and feel jealous. This could lead them to deciding to compete with the programme group "just to show them" how well they can do. Sometimes, in contexts like these, the participants are even encouraged by well-meaning teachers or administrators to compete with each other.

If the rivalry between groups affects posttest performance, it could maker it more difficult to detect the effects of the programme. As with diffusion and imitation, this threat generally works to in the direction of equalising the posttest performance across groups, increasing the chance that you won't see a programme effect, even if the programme is effective.

Resentful demoralisation

This is almost the opposite of compensatory rivalry. Here, students in the comparison group know what the programme group is getting. But here, instead of developing a rivalry, they get discouraged or angry and they give up (sometimes referred to as the "screw you" effect!). Unlike the previous two threats, this one is likely to exaggerate posttest differences between groups, making your programme look even more effective than it actually is.

Compensatory equalisation of treatment

This is the only threat of the four that primarily involves the people who help manage the research context rather than the participants themselves. When programme and comparison group participants are aware of each other's conditions they may wish they were in the other group (depending on the perceived desirability of the programme it could work either way). Often they or their parents or teachers will put pressure on the administrators to have them reassigned to the other group. The administrators may begin to feel that the allocation of goods to the groups is not "fair" and may be pressured to or independently undertake to compensate one group for the perceived advantage of the other.

If the special math tutoring programme was being done with state-of-the-art computers, you can bet that the parents of the children assigned to the traditional non-computerised comparison group will pressure the principal to "equalise" the situation. Perhaps the principal will give the comparison group some other good, or let them have access to the computers for other subjects. If these "compensating" programmes equalise the groups on posttest performance, it will tend to work against your detecting an effective programme even when it does work. For instance, a compensatory programme might improve the self-esteem of the comparison group and eliminate your chance to discover whether the math programme would cause changes in self-esteem relative to traditional math training.

As long as we engage in applied social research we will have to deal with the realities of human interaction and its effect on the research process. The threats described here can often be minimized by constructing multiple groups that are not aware of each other (e.g., programme group from one school, comparison group from another) or by training administrators in the importance of preserving group membership and not instituting equalising programmes. But we will never be able to entirely eliminate the possibility that human interactions are making it more difficult for us to assess cause-effect relationships.

5

Qualitative Research Methods

Qualitative research can be defined as "multimethod in focus, involving an interpretive, naturalistic approach to its subject matter". If you feel that this is too vague, it is probably because what this term means is too various. To illustrate this concept, we will describe the characteristics of qualitative research. Because many authors have pointed out many different characteristics, and because it is not possible to summarise them all in such a small space as this, we will discuss only three that are regarded as important, especially to social work students.

Meanings from the inside: Qualitative researchers attempt to understand meanings that people give to their deeds or to social phenomena. In other words, researchers see people from the inside. For example, when you conduct interviews with users of a residential care house for people with physical disabilities, you will have pictures of how they feel about their ordinary lives in the house. How do they think of staying or working at the house? What sort of limitations do they notice about their residence? How do they deal with conflicts with care workers and roommates? What tacit rules cover their human relations? Such questions would be very interesting for social workers that want to improve their care houses from the viewpoints of the users.

Direct contacts: Quantitative researchers may be able to do surveys without direct contact with research objects: they can collect data by using hired and trained interviewers or by mailing out questionnaires. Qualitative researchers, on the other hand, often enter into the natural fields of people whom they study, and have face-to-face interviews with them. Because of this, qualitative research is sometimes called "fieldwork." Although this direct connectedness with people and their lives attracts social workers, it also gives rise to several ethical problems, which quantitative researchers may not face. These ethical problems will be dealt with later in this document.

Analytic Induction: Analytic induction is a major logic of qualitative research. The rule is: take one case, and develop a working hypothesis to explain it. After that, you take another case, and examine whether the hypothesis can explain the new case. If it fails, you should revise the hypothesis to explain both of the cases. Then, take the third, and repeat the same process of examining and revising the hypothesis.

When you do not need to revise the hypothesis further, and you expect that the hypothesis will fit any new cases you might take, you will have refined the hypothesis enough. As you may have noticed, your choice of cases to be examined has an important bearing on the trustworthiness of analytic induction and is related to the sampling procedures of qualitative research mentioned below. This approach has been developed most fully by Strauss and Corbin. Not all qualitative research follows this approach, but the inductive approach to design, fieldwork and analysis is one of the most influential characteristics of qualitative inquiry.

Philosophy on Qualitative Research

It is essential for qualitative researchers to be aware of

the influence of philosophy on strategies of research, because without knowledge of related philosophy, they are apt to be confused when analysing qualitative data. Much has been written regarding the ways in which philosophical positions feed through to influence approaches to qualitative research. Four philosophical paradigms have been identified. They include positivism, postpositivism, critical theory, and constructivism.

Positivism

Positivism is rarely evident in a fully developed form in contemporary research, but is most usually identified with quantitative research. According to positivism, the "objective" world exists independently of any perspectives of the researchers. Therefore, researchers must disclose the "objective" facts. The distinguishing feature of positivism is the absence of any distinction between reality (as things that exist) and knowledge of reality (as things that are recognised). This paradigm is present in a diluted form in some qualitative research.

Postpositivism

Postpositivism is a modified form of positivism that appeared after the end of World War II. It admits that human beings cannot perfectly understand reality, whereas with rigorous data collection and analysis, researchers can approach the truth. Postpositivist covers a range of positions so wide that it scarcely earns the name of a paradigm.

It is widely influential within qualitative research and covers positions as different as the grounded theory approach Herbert Blumer's brand of symbolic interactionism recent developments under the heading of scientific realism, and the detailed ways of analysing qualitative data devised by Miles and Huberman. One of us has discussed the significance of postpositivist positions more fully elsewhere.

Critical Theory

Critical theory under a narrow definition originated in the Frankfurt School, which was founded in Germany, during the pre-war years. In this document, however, we would use such a wide definition of Critical Theory that it would include the basic paradigms of any qualitative research directed at generating empowering or emancipatory social change directly through research.

In Japan, a well-known one based on this paradigm is probably feminist research. Critical ethnography and participatory action research are also related to this. Reality cannot be grasped without researcher bias that is caused by historical, political, societal, ethnic, or gender conditions. Research should be very much related to social values, while the realisation of social values is the purpose of research.

Constructivism

As with postpositivist, contructivism includes a wide span of positions, from those indistinguishable from post-positivist approaches to relativist positions. Lincoln and Guba are perhaps the best known advocates of constructivism, and they are well towards the relativist end of the continuum. Their critique of conventional inquiry positions has become well known.

On reality, they came to advocate multiple, socially constructed realities which, "when known more fully, tend to produce diverging inquiry". Realities cannot be studies "in pieces" but only holistically and in context. The traditional image of the relationship between knower and known, researcher and subject, was rejected. "Knower and known not only could not remain distanced and separated in the process of evaluation, but probably should not". Hence, "the relationship, when properly established, is one of respectful negotiation, joint control, and reciprocal learning". Finally, because there are no enduring, context-free truth statements, and all human behaviour is time and context bound, "we began to doubt seriously the possibility of generalisation from one site to the next".

Ways of Collecting Data

Ways of collecting data vary in qualitative research. Because our purpose is to outline qualitative research, we will describe three classic methods of collecting qualitative data: interviews, participatory observation, and documentary analysis. However, we should remember that these older methods have been challenged by newer arrivals such as analysis of visual images and sound.

Interviews

Rogers and Bouey point out, "Without a doubt, the most utilised data collection method in qualitative research studies is the interview." Many authors classify qualitative interviews into three types: structured interviews, unstructured interviews, and semi-structured interviews.

First, structured interviews: sometimes called standardised interviews, these are often used in quantitative research. In structured interviews, researchers ask the same set of questions, in the same order, using the same words, to different interviewees. Structured interviews are convenient for comparing different interviewees' answers to the same questions, and when a team of researchers is involved in conducting the interviews.

Second, unstructured interviews: also called informal conversational interviews, these interviews do not have any predetermined set of questions; instead the researchers and interviewees talk freely. Unstructured interviews are often used in combination with participatory observation and although they may look easy to conduct, novices usually find them difficult because the researchers have to generate and develop questions according to what the interviewees say.

Third, semi-structured interviews: sometimes called guided interviews, these are somewhere between structured and unstructured interviews in format in that the researchers prepare interview guides that consist of a set of questions. The guides allow researchers to generate their own questions to develop interesting areas of inquiry during the interviews. This type of interview is widely used as the qualitative interview.

All three types of interview can be used in combination. For example, after conducting structured interviews, researchers can conduct semi-structured interviews, and finally unstructured interviews or, conversely, they may start with unstructured interviews to relax the interviewees, and move to a semi-structured interview format.

Participant Observation

Participant observation has been described as "the most intimate and morally hazardous" form of social research. Patton has demonstrated that there are variations in observational methods. First, the extent of the researcher's participation can vary from full participation to onlooker observation.

Second, there is a continuum between overt and covert observations. In overt observations, people know they are being observed whereas in covert observations, they do not. One reason why covert observations are conducted is that people might behave differently when they know they are being observed. There is much ethical discussion about covert observations in particular about the difficulties in deciding the extent to which the observations should be overt or covert.

Despite these difficulties, observations are powerful tools for researchers. For example, researcher visiting the setting to conduct interviews may unintentionally uncover much interesting data and many themes while waiting for interviewees to arrive. Even if you plan to use only interview data, visiting and observing the setting in which the interviewees are located must help you find important topics around the research. You might notice something that nobody has talked about in your interviews because it is so familiar to them that they think it unworthy to refer to or they may simply not want to talk about it.

Documentary Analysis

There are usually many documents associated with our research settings. According to Burgess, there are three sorts of distinctions among documents. One is made between primary sources and secondary sources. Primary sources have a direct relationship with those who are studied. They include letters, diaries, and reports. Although these documents describe first-hand accounts of situations, we should not accept them uncritically and "it is essential to locate them in context." where they were produced.

On the other hand, secondary sources are transcribed or edited from primary sources, and we should remember that they may include errors that the transcribing and editing processes made. Another distinction is made between public and private documents. For example, in a residential home for children, the public documents would include newsletters and books published by the organisation running the home about their history.

Private documents would include the children's diaries, and letters written by children to their parents and vice versa. Among public documents, for social work researchers, official documents records may be important. They include case files and staff diaries that social workers share as information resources for treatment. The third distinction is made between solicited and unsolicited documents.

Solicited documents are produced with requests of the researchers. For example, researchers can ask users of a social service to keep diaries in which users jot down whatever come into their mind. Unsolicited documents are naturally produced and later taken by researchers. They include personal diaries and letters.

Methods of Analysing Data

As mentioned above, there are several different philosophical backgrounds to qualitative research. The different bases of epistemology give rise to a wide variety of ways of analysing data, and therefore we will put forward very general principles or rules for analysing qualitative data.

Analyse the Data while Collecting Them

Unlike in quantitative research, data analysis in qualitative research can occur before the data collection process has been completed. Indeed, Coffey and Atkinson suggest that in qualitative research:

> We should never collect data without substantial analysis going on simultaneously. Letting data accumulate without preliminary analysis along the way is a recipe for unhappiness, if not total disaster.

In unstructured interviews, for instance, you should start to analyse what is being said while talking with people, otherwise, you will not be able to decide what questions to ask next in the conversation. In qualitative research, doing data analysis while collecting data is called the "principle of interaction between data collection and analysis".

Moreover, it is important to remember that the researcher is not the only person engaging in such a simultaneous analysis. The person being interviewed is also engaging in what Holstein and Gubrium call "indigenous coding". That is, interviewees may also analyse what they say while being interviewed. The researchers should take this into their consideration when they start to analyse the interview data.

Be Aware of the Context

A researcher conducting an interview with social workers about work-related stress might notice that what the interviewees say in the interview rooms of their agency is quite different from what they say in a location where different social rules operate such as a restaurant. It may be very hard for the interviewees to describe their work-related stress in the very place that produces their stress. Or the interviewees might overstate particular aspects of their stress in order to make the conversation in the restaurants more interesting and entertaining. Thus, it is vital for qualitative researchers to consider the context in which the data are obtained.

The importance of context has been brought to the forefront through the general availability of extensive electronic text manipulation in qualitative data analysis, as Seale pointed out. In other words, when "cut-and-paste techniques" (techniques for cutting off relevant segments and pasting them together) are applied to the analysis of "interview transcripts" (verbal and non-verbal records of interviews), consequently novice researchers often pay attention to the fragments of the transcript, and lose sight of the context in which the fragment is located, which can be misleading.

Be Reflexive

Many authors say, "In qualitative research, the investigator serves as a kind of 'instrument' in the collection and analysis of data". This means that reflexivity is an important aspect of qualitative research. According to Hammersley and Atkinson, reflexivity implies that "the orientations of researchers will be shaped by their socio-historical locations, including the values and interests that these locations confer upon them."

One way to become aware of one's own values and preconceptions is to use "a cultural review." For example, Shaw gives the illustration of a researcher "preparing to interview a woman having difficulties coping with caring for her son of 25 who has serious learning disabilities and lives at home".

The researcher could make a self-inquiry by asking the following questions: "Who have I cared for?" what would be "my own feelings about being cared for by a close relative?" and "my reaction to carrying out personal care tasks" and so on. Another way of being reflexive is to keep "a reflexive journal" in which researchers put "information about their schedule and logistics, insights, and reasons for methodological decisions".

Be Flexible

As Coffey and Atkinson have repeatedly mentioned, "There are many ways of analysing qualitative data.... We certainly want to discourage our readers from uncritically adopting particular approaches to analysis without making principled decisions from among the available alternatives." In particular, they worry about the misconception that the way to analyse data is to use some form of coding and "stress... that although coding may be part of the process of analysis, it should not be thought of as the analysis in itself".

Make your Decisions Clear

In their reports, researchers should describe what decisions were made and actions were taken through the analysing processes. Many novice researchers using qualitative research say, for example, "Through qualitative interviews I have derived such and such a concept," without clarifying the decisions they made during the analysis.

As Miles and Huberman have mentioned, however, "Keeping a precise record of the actual criteria and decision rules used...is essential". An example of a simple decision rule given by Miles and Huberman is "two confirmations and no contradiction". When applying this rule to qualitative interviews, researchers would regard a concept as important if it is confirmed by at least two interviewees and negated by nobody.

Quotes Supporting Your Ideas

One of the basis rules in writing a qualitative interview report is to use quotes of the interview transcripts that support your ideas. How to edit and use quotes is, however, a rather difficult task for novices.

Kvale introduces the following guidelines for reporting interview quotes: First, the quotes should be linked to the related text. Second, the contexts of the quotes should be clarified. Third, the quotes should be given interpretation, otherwise the readers cannot understand why they are quoted. Fourth, a proper balance between quotes and text should be kept. When the first three principles are neglected one result is that a surfeit of half-digested quotations dominates the text. Fifth, the quotes should usually be relatively short in length.

Long quotes are often vague in their meaning. However, Atkinson has demonstrated the value of longer quotations as contextualising narrative. Sixth, only the most illustrative quotes should be presented. Too many quotes and too much repetition makes a report dull. Seventh, "interview quotes should be rendered in a written style." We are not sure how strictly this rule should be applied to Japanese editing because in the Japanese language there seems to be wider differences between written and spoken styles than in Kvale's language.

However, it is important to edit all quotes sufficiently so that readers of the report can understand them easily. Lastly, Kvale emphasises that "In order that the reader will know about the extent of editing of the quotes, the principles for editing should be given, preferably with a simple list of symbols for pauses, omissions, and the like.".

Forms of Results

Having accumulated a huge amount of transcripts, students often ask us what they should find through their analysis. To put it very simply, successful qualitative research reports often include new concepts, new typology, or new causal networks.

Conceptualisation

As Hammersley and Atkinson point out, "The initial task in analysing qualitative data is to find some concepts that help us to make sense of what is going on in the scenes documented by the data." This process is often called "conceptualisation." New concepts may be taken from "folk terms" which are used in the culture of the interviewees, or the researchers may find useful concepts though literature reviews on the subjects. A familiar example of the power of conceptualisation is Goffman's work on "stigma" and "total institutions".

By listing concepts and relating them to one other, we can produces typologies. An example is shown below. Social work practitioners appear to be strongly preoccupied with accountability. Research has elicited recurring instances of ways in which practice regarded by social workers as having not gone well is likely to trigger deep uncertainties in the mind of the reflective practitioner.

This research suggests there was a widespread sense that outcomes, both positive and negative, were beyond prediction, and will never cease to jump out and surprise the practitioner. An example of a typology has been developed by Bull and Shaw to illustrate the accounts that may be adopted by social workers in relation to actions and events for which they may be called to account.

Matrices

A matrix is a useful form for displaying typologies. The following example was produced, in research that Oka participated in, when leaders of parent groups were asked what they regarded as the most important of their activities. This question was asked of over twenty leaders, and only those concepts were selected when they were included in the quotes of two or more interviewees.

Matrices are also useful for describing or explaining situations, time-ordered changes, and relations between two lists of concepts and so on. Miles and Huberman introduced sophisticated techniques of matrices for display of qualitative data.

Networks

It is commonly argued that qualitative data are used for generating hypotheses, or describing process, whereas quantitative data are used to analyse outcomes or verify hypotheses. We believe that this division of labour is rigid and limiting. Having said this, the division is reinforced by the frequent absence of discussions of cause in qualitative methodology and analysis texts.

Qualitative evaluation cannot resolve the problems of causal conclusions any more than quantitative evaluation, but it can assess causality "as it actually plays out in a particular setting". As well as matrices, networks are a good way of displaying data and causalit because they can describe complex stories in a simple way. The following is adapted from a research report one of whose authors is Oka: this is a causal network on the shortage of group leaders in self-help groups for parents whose children have rare and serious diseases.

Ethical Issues

Ethical issues related to social work research are very important and have been much discussed. All qualitative researchers in social work should give serious thoughts to these issues particularly as the nature of qualitative research adds its own complications. In this document, we will deal with some ethical issues pertaining to qualitative research. They include confidentiality, informed consent, emotional safety, and reciprocity.

Confidentiality

Very few people would willingly express their most

private details, opinions and emotions in public documents knowing that their names would be published. Thus, confidentiality is a vital requirement for credible research.

More importantly, mere anonymity is insufficient for confidentiality to be safeguarded. For example, suppose a paper says, "We visited a university-attached day care centre for people with mental disabilities in City Y, Prefecture K." If the author's office is in the Kanto Area, readers can readily assume Prefecture K to be Kanagawa Prefecture. They might also associate City Y with Yokohama City, the second largest city in Japan.

Even a large city does has not very many university-attached day care centres, consequently although this paper may have concealed the name of the site, it fails to maintain confidentiality. If this paper includes quotes from service users who criticise professionals very strongly, the professionals may suspect that certain of their own clients are the critics. Suspicion such as this can only harm people, consequently, in particular those who are socially disadvantaged.

Qualitative researchers require prolonged engagement in the field in order to carry out effective research. If you conduct research at Hospital A for some years and publish a qualitative case report on an anonymous hospital, many people around you will surely conclude that the hospital mentioned in the report is Hospital A. In this case, you should pay as much attention as possible to maintaining the confidentiality of the individual participants, changing the facts where necessary as long as these changes do not distort the essential elements of the report.

6

Quantitative Research Methods

The impacts of a development intervention are often difficult to quantify. That is no reason for not quantifying them. If the objectives of the intervention are strictly qualitative, that may be a better reason. Even then however, some degree of quantification may be necessary in order to assess the extent to which the intervention has succeeded. If the sole aim of a project is to change the colour of a building from dilapidated rust to sparkling blue, the change is strictly qualitative. However, the ultimate impact is not the colour but people's response to it.

The assessor may need to find out how many people like it, how many dislike it, what numbers of people of what sorts fall in which category, and where their response fits on a scale from love to hate. As discussed in the Core Text, the terms of reference of an impact assessment may be restricted to observing the achievement or otherwise of intermediary goals rather than ultimate effects. Like the colour of a building, those intermediary goals may be qualitative. If however the assessment aims to determine the ultimate effects on stakeholders, the assessment usually needs to be quantified if it is to be meaningful.

As well as providing an understanding of mechanisms through which results are achieved, the assessment must focus on those results, and ensure that judgements are based on reliable, factual information. Broadly speaking, most impact assessments need to use a combination of quantitative, qualitative and participatory techniques. This is generally the case whether the prime aim of the assessment is to learn lessons, or to establish accountability.

Lesson learning 'aims to understand why particular aid activities are more or less successful, in order to improve future performance'. The phrase 'more or less' is itself a quantification, which has to be carried out before lessons can be learned. Quantitative techniques endeavour to measure actual impacts. Qualitative ones evaluate how and why those impacts occur. Participatory approaches involve stakeholders in either type of evaluation. The mix of techniques that is most appropriate will depend on the nature of the intervention, and of the impact assessment. In most cases if not all, some degree of quantification will be necessary.

Quantification of impacts can be extraordinarily difficult, if not impossible, without information on the baseline situation in the absence of the intervention. For this reason, impact assessment should be taken into account within project design, so that gathering the necessary information can begin at the beginning. If an intervention has a strong research element to it, baseline information may be monitored throughout the intervention, by observing any changes for a control group that is unaffected by the intervention itself. This will give an indication of the effects of extraneous factors.

Otherwise, baseline information is at least needed for the situation before the intervention began. If such information is not gathered as part of project preparation, or within a project itself, an impact assessment may have some difficulty in backtracking to try and find it. Ideally, the impact assessment methodology should be designed at the same time as the intervention itself is designed, to identify appropriate indicators within the logframe, and determine initial values before the intervention begins.

The project team, with the participation of stakeholders where appropriate, will monitor changes in indicators from their baseline values as the project progresses, and will at the same time be alert to any unexpected impacts. The prime purpose of monitoring will be to learn and adapt in order to maximise the value of the intervention. However, this monitoring will also contribute considerably to any external impact assessment. If the project's own monitoring results are recorded, along with the lessons learned and the actions taken, external evaluation can in some cases reduce to a simple quality assurance and information dissemination exercise.

The evaluation will check that monitoring has been conducted appropriately, and if necessary carry out limited independent checks, but otherwise the monitoring results may be taken as they stand. Likewise, the evaluation will review the lessons learned by the project team, and if necessary conduct additional investigations of unexpected effects, but otherwise the lessons disseminated by the evaluation will be those learned within the project itself.

In the context of microcredit activities for example, full integration of this nature may be regarded as the integration of impact assessment with the programme's own market research. At the opposite extreme, when no monitoring is undertaken within the project, or if it is not recorded, or if it has not been planned with impact assessment in mind, external evaluation becomes more of an inquisition. It has to dig back to find qualitative and quantitative information on the baseline situation, dig behind opinions expressed by the project team to get at objective evidence, and involve stakeholders in independent participatory activities.

The lessons that are disseminated will be those learned from the evaluation, rather than those learned within the intervention itself. This problem of lack of baseline information is evident in some of the case studies shown on this site, eg AGENT in Zimbabwe, and Mineworkers' Development Agency (MDA) in South Africa. Partly this is a historical problem in that at the time these projects were started less attention was paid to the institution of impact assessment at the design stage. Between these two extremes, internal monitoring and external evaluation can integrate with each other and complement each other while performing different roles.

It may be unnecessary to monitor any more than a few key factors on a continuous basis, leaving a wider range of impacts to be evaluated at specific points in the programme. Additional effort and/or specialist expertise may be required for this, either as an impact assessment commissioned as part of the intervention, or as an independent evaluation of it. At the very least however, the indicators that will be used for impact assessment should be chosen at the outset, and their baseline values should be determined during project preparation and/or from the earliest stages of implementation.

Goal of an Intervention

The overall goal of an intervention is likely to be quantitative. Its specific purpose may be a qualitative change leading to that goal, and its planned outputs may similarly be largely qualitative. The qualitative aspects of an impact assessment will need to be designed so as to give a good understanding of those qualitative changes, in relation to what is planned. Its quantitative aspects need to measure the extent to which the planned changes have been achieved—totally, partially, not at all, or even the opposite effect to that intended.

The quantitative aspects may also aim to measure the extent to which the qualitative changes that have occurred do in fact contribute to the goal. The route from goal, to purpose, to outputs, to indicators that will measure them, and finally to the data that need to be collected in an impact assessment. The methods used in the impact assessment, the indicators, and the key information collected have been designed to satisfy this need for quantitative information. Note also that a baseline study was carried out with the aim of enabling communities themselves to monitor change over time. In this case, the level of integration of impact assessment into the intervention itself extended to continuous participation by stakeholders.

Sustainable Livelihoods and Human Rights Approaches

Neither the sustainable livelihoods nor the human rights approaches to development interventions obviate the need for quantification of impacts.

The human rights approach highlights the need for a stakeholder analysis to identify social groups whose rights may be affected. For those groups, impact assessment will need to quantify, as far as possible, impacts on:

- increased incomes and standards of living
- employment creation
- economic independence of poor people
- health and well-being
- security and social protection
- skills acquisition and access to information
- political and cultural participation

Impact of Quantitative Assessment

Obtaining and using quantitative information which will lead to a thorough understanding of the impacts of an intervention may entail a carefully designed methodology covering the entire impact assessment exercise. This may include:

- designing the overall review questions
- defining the key issues
- assessing the significance of different types of impact
- deciding when livelihood impacts do not need to be quantified
- obtaining baseline data
- undertaking desk research
- data collection approaches and methods
- integrating impact monitoring into the intervention

Analysis of Quantitative Information

Some types of quantitative information speaks for itself, such as when a stakeholder group shows a marked increase in incomes compared with a clearly comparable control group. In other cases fairly sophisticated statistical analysis may be necessary in order to draw any reliable conclusions.

In theory, the confidence limits which can be calculated by statistical analysis should show how reliable the findings are. In practice, undetected systematic errors in the data can far outweigh the known uncertainties. The findings can then have a semblance of scientific rigour which is totally unjustified. Meanwhile, purely qualitative techniques can suffer from a high degree of subjectivity. Where the potential for systematic errors is high, quantitative techniques entailing sophisticated statistical analyses may be less cost-effective, and in the end less reliable, than a combination of much simpler quantitative and qualitative methods.

In attempting to disentangle all the complex interactions between the causes and effects which influence people's livelihoods, and to assess just how large and how significant the impacts of an intervention are, the most important thing is to ask the right questions, of the right people, including the impact assessor, in the way that best elicits honest and open response.

7

Social Work Research Evaluation

The primary job of the evaluator is to examine rigorously the impact of interventions. However, a secondary job is to persuade those who believe that they can determine their effectiveness by looking into their clients' eyes to be more critical of the role that their services play in their clients' lives. Although clients' eyes may reflect gratitude, they cannot reveal whether a programme reaches its intended target population, or whether clients would have been just as well off without the programme. A critical perspective is needed if the efforts are to continually improve over time.

We are at a cusp of change in the way that programmes are funded and delivered. Governmental funding, even for the most basic needs such as housing and food, is drying up, and more reliance is being placed on the non-profit sector. Increasingly, government is relying on the non-profit sector, with its army of volunteers and relatively low—paid staff, to compensate for gaps in governmental programmes. This became painfully evident during the aftermath of Hurricane Katrina, when short—term federal assistance seemed ineffective, and government officials asked Americans to donate to a host of non-profit organisations for hurricane aftermath relief initiatives because the federal government did not provide enough support to meet the tremendous need that developed.

However, with more reliance placed on the non-profit sector comes the demand for all non-profit organisations (also known in the international context as nongovernmental organisations or NGOs), and especially those that compete with other non-profits for " market share, " to demonstrate their effectiveness. This demand derives from many sources. First, government and consumers would like to know which non-profits are most effective at providing comparable services. In this respect, evaluation is viewed as essentially a means of providing information to rank programmes and organisations. Second, there exists curiosity about the ultimate effectiveness of services and programmes; in this regard, evaluation is used to determine which approaches are the most appropriate for remedying a problem or for bringing about change.

Although well trained in service delivery, many in the non-profit world lack training in the nuances of evaluation research. Likewise, many in the funding world who have " caught the evaluation bug " lack the background to determine how to form fair criteria by which to judge and reward effective non-profit organisations and programmes. Working in the background behind service deliverers and funders are people who call themselves evaluators.

Many evaluators are primarily trained in a field other than evaluation, such as public health, sociology, economics, statistics, or public policy. They may have had some formal training in evaluation, but they often have moved into evaluation over time (sometimes because of job and market demands) and many have acquired mostly on—the - job training. For this reason, although the majority of evaluators have in common a desire to learn the " truth " about interventions, they bring to the table a divergent set of skills and may place varying emphases on different aspects of programmes, policies, and evaluatory practices.

Evaluation Framework

The following are the steps to successfully develop an evaluation of a programme.

1. Are the evaluation activities formative or summative?
2. What questions are in the universe of possible evaluation questions?
3. Rigorously describe the program by developing the program theory and using a program logic model.
4. Revisit and narrow the universe of evaluation questions.
5. Develop the evaluation plan.
6. Develop a data collection and data analysis plan.
7. Analyze the data.
8. Write evaluation report.

8

Survey Research

Survey research is one of the most important areas of measurement in applied social research. The broad area of survey research encompasses any measurement procedures that involve asking questions of respondents. A "survey" can be anything form a short paper-and-pencil feedback form to an intensive one-on-one in-depth interview.

We'll begin by looking at the different types of surveys that are possible. These are roughly divided into two broad areas: Questionnaires and Interviews. Next, we'll look at how you select the survey method that is best for your situation.

Once you've selected the survey method, you have to construct the survey itself. Here, we will be address a number of issues including: the different types of questions; decisions about question content; decisions about question wording; decisions about response format; and, question placement and sequence in your instrument. We turn next to some of the special issues involved in administering a personal interview. Finally, we'll consider some of the advantages and disadvantages of survey methods.

Kinds of Surveys

Surveys can be divided into two broad categories: the questionnaire and the interview. Questionnaires are usually paper-and-pencil instruments that the respondent completes. Interviews are completed by the interviewer based on the respondent says. Sometimes, it's hard to tell the difference between a questionnaire and an interview. For instance, some people think that questionnaires always ask short closed-ended questions while interviews always ask broad open-ended ones. But you will see questionnaires with open-ended questions and there will often be a series of closed-ended questions asked in an interview.

Survey research has changed dramatically in the last ten years. We have automated telephone surveys that use random dialing methods. There are computerised kiosks in public places that allows people to ask for input. A whole new variation of group interview has evolved as focus group methodology. Increasingly, survey research is tightly integrated with the delivery of service. Your hotel room has a survey on the desk.

Questionnaires

When most people think of questionnaires, they think of the mail survey. All of us have, at one time or another, received a questionnaire in the mail. There are many advantages to mail surveys. They are relatively inexpensive to administer. You can send the exact same instrument to a wide number of people. They allow the respondent to fill it out at their own convenience. But there are some disadvantages as well. Response rates from mail surveys are often very low. And, mail questionnaires are not the best vehicles for asking for detailed written responses.

A second type is the group administered questionnaire. A sample of respondents is brought together and asked to respond to a structured sequence of questions. Traditionally, questionnaires were administered in group settings for convenience. The researcher could give the questionnaire to those who were present and be fairly sure that there would be a high response rate. If the respondents were unclear about the meaning of a question they could ask for clarification. And, there were often organisational settings where it was relatively easy to assemble the group (in a company or business, for instance).

What's the difference between a group administered questionnaire and a group interview or focus group? In the group administered questionnaire, each respondent is handed an instrument and asked to complete it while in the room. Each respondent completes an instrument. In the group interview or focus group, the interviewer facilitates the session. People work as a group, listening to each other's comments and answering the questions. Someone takes notes for the entire group—people don't complete an interview individually.

A less familiar type of questionnaire is the household drop-off survey. In this approach, a researcher goes to the respondent's home or business and hands the respondent the instrument. In some cases, the respondent is asked to mail it back or the interview returns to pick it up. This approach attempts to blend the advantages of the mail survey and the group administered questionnaire. Like the mail survey, the respondent can work on the instrument in private, when it's convenient. Like the group administered questionnaire, the interviewer makes personal contact with the respondent—they don't just send an impersonal survey instrument. And, the respondent can ask questions about the study and get clarification on what is to be done.

Generally, this would be expected to increase the percent of people who are willing to respond.

Types of Survey Methods

Selecting the type of survey you are going to use is one of the most critical decisions in many social research contexts. You'll see that there are very few simple rules that will make the decision for you—have to use your judgment to balance the advantages and disadvantages of different survey types.

Population Issues

The first set of considerations have to do with the population and its accessibility.

Can the population be enumerated?

For some population, you have a complete listing of the units that will be sampled. For others, such a list is difficult or impossible to compile. For instance, there are complete listings of registered voters or person with active drivers licenses. But no one keeps a complete list of homeless people. If you are doing a study that requires input from homeless persons, you are very likely going to need to go and find the respondents personally. In such contexts, you can pretty much rule out the idea of mail surveys or telephone interviews.

Is the population literate?

Questionnaires require that your respondents can read. While this might seem initially like a reasonable assumption for many adult population, we know from recent research that the instance of adult illiteracy is alarmingly high. And, even if your respondents can read to some degree, your questionnaire may contain difficult or technical vocabulary. Clearly, there are some population that you would expect to be illiterate. Young children would not be good targets for questionnaires.

Are there language issues?

We live in a multilingual world. Virtually every society has members who speak other than the predominant language. Some countries (like Canada) are officially multilingual. And, our increasingly global economy requires us to do research that spans countries and language groups. Can you produce multiple versions of your questionnaire? For mail instruments, can you know in advance the language your respondent speaks, or do you send multiple translations of your instrument? Can you be confident that important connotations in your instrument are not culturally specific? Could some of the important nuances get lost in the process of translating your questions?

Will the population cooperate?

People who do research on immigration issues have a difficult methodological problem. They often need to speak with undocumented immigrants or people who may be able to identify others who are. Why would we expect those respondents to cooperate? Although the researcher may mean no harm, the respondents are at considerable risk legally if information they divulge should get into the hand of the authorities. The same can be said for any target group that is engaging in illegal or unpopular activities.

What are the geographic restrictions?

Is your population of interest dispersed over too broad a geographic range for you to study feasibly with a personal interview? It may be possible for you to send a mail instrument to a nationwide sample. You may be able to conduct phone interviews with them. But it will almost certainly be less feasible to do research that requires interviewers to visit directly with respondents if they are widely dispersed.

Important Sampling Issues

The sample is the actual group you will have to contact in some way. There are several important sampling issues you need to consider when doing survey research.

What data is available?

What information do you have about your sample? Do you know their current addresses? Their current phone numbers? Are your contact lists up to date?

Can respondents be found?

Can your respondents be located? Some people are very busy. Some travel a lot. Some work the night shift. Even if you have an accurate phone or address, you may not be able to locate or make contact with your sample.

Who is the respondent?

Who is the respondent in your study? Let's say you draw a sample of households in a small city. A household is not a respondent. Do you want to interview a specific individual? Do you want to talk only to the "head of household" (and how is that person defined)? Are you willing to talk to any member of the household? Do you state that you will speak to the first adult member of the household who opens the door? What if that person is unwilling to be interviewed but someone else in the house is willing? How do you deal with multi-family households? Similar problems arise when you sample groups, agencies, or companies. Can you survey any member of the organisation? Or, do you only want to speak to the Director of Human Resources? What if the person you would like to interview is unwilling or unable to participate? Do you use another member of the organisation?

Can all members of population be sampled?

If you have an incomplete list of the population (i.e., sampling frame) you may not be able to sample every member of the population. Lists of various groups are extremely hard to keep up to date. People move or change their names. Even though they are on your sampling frame listing, you may not be able to get to them. And, it's possible they are not even on the list.

Are response rates likely to be a problem?

Even if you are able to solve all of the other population and sampling problems, you still have to deal with the issue of response rates. Some members of your sample will simply refuse to respond. Others have the best of intentions, but can't seem to find the time to send in your questionnaire by the due date. Still others misplace the instrument or forget about the appointment for an interview. Low response rates are among the most difficult of problems in survey research. They can ruin an otherwise well-designed survey effort.

Question Issues

Sometimes the nature of what you want to ask respondents will determine the type of survey you select.

What types of questions can be asked?

Are you going to be asking personal questions? Are you going to need to get lots of detail in the responses? Can you anticipate the most frequent or important types of responses and develop reasonable closed-ended questions?

How complex will the questions be?

Sometimes you are dealing with a complex subject or topic. The questions you want to ask are going to have multiple parts. You may need to branch to sub-questions.

Will screening questions be needed?

A screening question may be needed to determine whether the respondent is qualified to answer your question of interest. For instance, you wouldn't want to ask someone their opinions about a specific computer programme without first "screening" them to find out whether they have any experience using the programme. Sometimes you have to screen on several variables (e.g., age, gender, experience). The more complicated the screening, the less likely it is that you can rely on paper-and-pencil instruments without confusing the respondent.

Can question sequence be controlled?

Is your survey one where you can construct in advance a reasonable sequence of questions? Or, are you doing an initial exploratory study where you may need to ask lots of follow-up questions that you can't easily anticipate?

Will lengthy questions be asked?

If your subject matter is complicated, you may need to give the respondent some detailed background for a question. Can you reasonably expect your respondent to sit still long enough in a phone interview to ask your question?

Will long response scales be used?

If you are asking people about the different computer equipment they use, you may have to have a lengthy response list (CD-ROM drive, floppy drive, mouse, touch pad, modem, network connection, external speakers, etc.). Clearly, it may be difficult to ask about each of these in a short phone interview.

Content Issues

The content of your study can also pose challenges for the different survey types you might utilise.

Can the respondents be expected to know about the issue?

If the respondent does not keep up with the news, they may not even know about the news issue you want to ask them about. Or, if you want to do a study of family finances and you are talking to the spouse who doesn't pay the bills on a regular basis, they may not have the information to answer your questions.

Will respondent need to consult records?

Even if the respondent understands what you're asking about, you may need to allow them to consult their records in order to get an accurate answer. For instance, if you ask them how much money they spent on food in the past month, they may need to look up their personal check and credit card records. In this case, you don't want to be involved in an interview where they would have to go look things up while they keep you waiting (they wouldn't be comfortable with that).

Bias Issues

People come to the research endeavour with their own sets of biases and prejudices. Sometimes, these biases will be less of a problem with certain types of survey approaches.

Can social desirability be avoided?

Respondents generally want to "look good" in the eyes of

others. None of us likes to look like we don't know an answer. We don't want to say anything that would be embarrassing. If you ask people about information that may put them in this kind of position, they may not tell you the truth, or they may "spin" the response so that it makes them look better. This may be more of a problem in an interview situation where they are face-to face or on the phone with a live interviewer.

Can interviewer distortion and subversion be controlled?

Interviewers may distort an interview as well. They may not ask questions that make them uncomfortable. They may not listen carefully to respondents on topics for which they have strong opinions. They may make the judgment that they already know what the respondent would say to a question based on their prior responses, even though that may not be true.

Can false respondents be avoided?

With mail surveys it may be difficult to know who actually responded. Did the head of household complete the survey or someone else? Did the CEO actually give the responses or instead pass the task off to a subordinate? Is the person you're speaking with on the phone actually who they say they are? At least with personal interviews, you have a reasonable chance of knowing who you are speaking with. In mail surveys or phone interviews, this may not be the case.

Administrative Issues

Last, but certainly not least, you have to consider the feasibility of the survey method for your study.

Costs

Cost is often the major determining factor in selecting survey type. You might prefer to do personal interviews, but can't justify the high cost of training and paying for the interviewers. You may prefer to send out an extensive mailing but can't afford the postage to do so.

Facilities

Do you have the facilities (or access to them) to process and manage your study? In phone interviews, do you have well-equipped phone surveying facilities? For focus groups, do you have a comfortable and accessible room to host the group? Do you have the equipment needed to record and transcribe responses?

Time

Some types of surveys take longer than others. Do you need responses immediately (as in an overnight public opinion poll)? Have you budgeted enough time for your study to send out mail surveys and follow-up reminders, and to get the responses back by mail? Have you allowed for enough time to get enough personal interviews to justify that approach?

Personnel

Different types of surveys make different demands of personnel. Interviews require interviewers who are motivated and well-trained. Group administered surveys require people who are trained in group facilitation. Some studies may be in a technical area that requires some degree of expertise in the interviewer.

Clearly, there are lots of issues to consider when you are selecting which type of survey you wish to use in your study. And there is no clear and easy way to make this decision in many contexts. There may not be one approach which is clearly the best. You may have to make trade-offs of advantages and disadvantages. There is judgment involved. Two expert researchers may, for the very same problem or issue, select entirely different survey methods. But, if you select a method that isn't appropriate or doesn't fit the context, you can doom a study before you even begin designing the instruments or questions themselves.

Survey Construction

Constructing a survey instrument is an art in itself. There are numerous small decisions that must be made—about content, wording, format, placement—that can have important consequences for your entire study. While there's no one perfect way to accomplish this job, we do have lots of advice to offer that might increase your chances of developing a better final product.

First of all you'll learn about the two major types of surveys that exist, the questionnaire and the interview and the different varieties of each. Then you'll see how to write questions for surveys. There are three areas involved in writing a question:

- determining the question content, scope and purpose
- choosing the response format that you use for collecting information from the respondent
- figuring out how to word the question to get at the issue of interest

Finally, once you have your questions written, there is the issue of how best to place them in your survey. You'll see that although there are many aspects of survey construction that are just common sense, if you are not careful you can make critical errors that have dramatic effects on your results.

Question Content

For each question in your survey, you should ask yourself how well it addresses the content you are trying to get at. Here are some content-related questions you can ask about your survey questions.

Examine each question

Examine each question to see if you need to ask it at all and if you need to ask it at the level of detail you currently have.

— Do you need the age of each child or just the number of children under 16?

— Do you need to ask income or can you estimate?

Several questions needed

This is the classic problem of the double-barrelled question. You should think about splitting each of the following questions into two separate ones. You can often spot these kinds of problems by looking for the conjunction "and" in your question.

— What are your feelings towards African-Americans and Hispanic-Americans?

— What do you think of proposed changes in benefits and hours?

Another reason you might need more than one question is that the question you ask does not cover all possibilities. For instance, if you ask about earnings, the respondent might not mention all income (e.g., dividends, gifts). Or, if you ask the respondents if they're in favour of public TV, they might not understand that you're asking generally. They may not be in favour of public TV for themselves (they never watch it), but might favour it very much for their children (who watch Sesame Street regularly). You might be better off asking two questions, one for their own viewing and one for other members of their household.

Sometimes you need to ask additional questions because your question does not give you enough context to interpret the answer. For instance, if you ask about attitudes towards Catholics, can you interpret this without finding out about their attitudes towards religion in general, or other religious groups?

At times, you need to ask additional questions because your question does not determine the intensity of the respondent's attitude or belief. For example, if they say they support public TV, you probably should also ask them whether they ever watch it or if they would be willing to have their tax dollars spent on it. It's one thing for a respondent to tell you they support something. But the intensity of that response is greater if they are willing to back their sentiment of support with their behaviour.

Needed information

Look at each question in your survey to see whether the respondent is likely to have the necessary information to be able to answer the question. For example, let's say you want to ask the question:

Do you think dean rusk acted correctly in the bay of Pigs crisis?

The respondent won't be able to answer this question if they have no idea who Dean Rusk was or what the Bay of Pigs crisis was. In surveys of television viewing, you cannot expect that the respondent can answer questions about shows they have never watched. You should ask a filter question first before asking them their opinions about it.

The question need to be more specific

Sometimes we ask our questions too generally and the information we obtain is more difficult to interpret. For example, let's say you want to find out respondent's opinions about a specific book. You could ask them

How well did you like the book?

on some scale ranging from "Not At All" to "Extremely Well." But what would their response mean? What does it mean to say you liked a book very well? Instead, you might as questions designed to be more specific like:

— Did you recommend the book to others? or

— Did you look for other books by that author?

Question Sufficiently General

You can err in the other direction as well by being too specific. For instance, if you ask someone to list the televisions programme they liked best in the past week, you could get a very different answer than if you asked them which show they've enjoyed most over the past year.

Perhaps a show they don't usually like had a great episode in the past week, or their show was pre-empted by another programme.

Question Biased

One danger in question-writing is that your own biases and blind-spots may affect the wording. For instance, you might generally be in favour of tax cuts. If you ask a question like:

What do you see as the benefits of a tax cut?

you're only asking about one side of the issue. You might get a very different picture of the respondents' positions if you also asked about the disadvantages of tax cuts. The same thing could occur if you are in favour of public welfare and you ask:

What do you see as the disadvantages of eliminating welfare?

without also asking about the potential benefits.

Respondent Answer Truthfully

For each question on your survey, ask yourself whether the respondent will have any difficulty answering the question truthfully. If there is some reason why they may not, consider rewording the question. For instance, some people are sensitive about answering questions about their exact age or income. In this case, you might give them response brackets to choose from. Sometimes even bracketed responses won't be enough.

Some people do not like to share how much money they give to charitable causes (they may be afraid of being solicited even more). No matter how you word the question, they would not be likely to tell you their contribution rate.

But sometimes you can do this by posing the question in terms of a hypothetical projective respondent (a little bit like a projective test). In this case, you might get reasonable estimates if you ask the respondent how much money "people you know" typically give in a year to charitable causes. Finally, you can sometimes dispense with asking a question at all if you can obtain the answer unobtrusively. If you are interested in finding out what magazines the respondent reads, you might instead tell them you are collecting magazines for a recycling drive and ask if they have any old ones to donate.

Question Wording

One of the major difficulty in writing good survey questions is getting the wording right. Even slight wording differences can confuse the respondent or lead to incorrect interpretations of the question.

Question Misunderstood

The survey author has to always be on the lookout for questions that could be misunderstood or confusing. For instance, if you ask a person for their nationality, it might not be clear what you want. Or, if you ask for marital status, do you want someone to say simply that they are either married or no married? Or, do you want more detail (like divorced, widow/widower, etc.)? Some terms are just to vague to be useful. For instance, if you ask a question about the "mass media," what do you mean? The newspapers? Radio? Television? Here's one of my favourites. Let's say you want to know the following:

What kind of headache remedy do you use?

Do you want to know what brand name medicine they take? Do you want to know about "home" remedies? Are you asking whether they prefer a pill, capsule or caplet?

Make a Question

Sometimes we don't stop to consider how a question will appear from the respondent's point-of-view. We don't think about the assumptions behind our questions. For instance, if you ask what social class someone's in, you assume that they know what social class is and that they think of themselves as being in one. In this kind of case, you may need to use a filter question first to determine whether either of these assumptions is true.

Time Frame Specified

Whenever you use the words "will", "could", "might", or "may" in a question, you might suspect that the question asks a time-related question. Be sure that, if it does, you have specified the time frame precisely. For instance, you might ask:

– Do you think Congress will cut taxes? or something like
– Do you think Congress could successfully resist tax cuts?

Neither of these questions specifies a time frame.

Personal is the Wording

With a change of just a few words, a question can go from being relatively impersonal to probing into your private perspectives. Consider the following three questions, each of which asks about the respondent's satisfaction with working conditions:

- Are working conditions satisfactory or not satisfactory in the plant where you work?
- Do you feel that working conditions satisfactory or not satisfactory in the plant where you work?
- Are you personally satisfied with working conditions in the plant where you work?

The first question is stated from a fairly detached, objective viewpoint. The second asks how you "feel." The last asks whether you are "personally satisfied." Be sure the questions in your survey are at an appropriate level for your context. And, be sure there is consistency in this across questions in your survey.

Asking Question too Directly

There are times when asking a question too directly may be too threatening or disturbing for respondents. For instance, consider a study where you want to discuss battlefield experiences with former soldiers who experienced trauma. Examine the following three question options:

- How did you feel about being in the war?
- How well did the equipment hold up in the field?
- How well were new recruits trained?

The first question may be too direct. For this population it may elicit powerful negative emotions based on their recollections. The second question is a less direct one. It asks about equipment in the field, but, for this population, may also lead the discussion toward more difficult issues to discuss directly. The last question is probably the least direct and least threatening. Bashing the new recruits is standard protocol in almost any social context. The question is likely to get the respondent talking, recounting anecdotes, without eliciting much stress. Of course, all of this may simply be begging the question. If you are doing a study where the respondents may experience high levels of stress because of the questions you ask, you should reconsider the ethics of doing the study.

Other Wording Issues

The nuances of language guarantee that the task of the question writer will be endlessly complex. Without trying to generate an exhaustive list, here are a few other questions to keep in mind:

— Does the question contain difficult or unclear terminology?
— Does the question make each alternative explicit?
— Is the wording objectionable?
— Is the wording loaded or slanted?

QUESTION PLACEMENT

Decisions About Placement

One of the most difficult tasks facing the survey designer involves the ordering of questions. Which topics should be introduced early in the survey, and which later? If you leave your most important questions until the end, you may find that your respondents are too tired to give them the kind of attention you would like. If you introduce them too early, they may not yet be ready to address the topic, especially if it is a difficult or disturbing one. There are no easy answers to these problems—you have to use your judgment. Whenever you think about question placement, consider the following questions:

- Is the answer influenced by prior questions?
- Does question come too early or too late to arouse interest?
- Does the question receive sufficient attention?

Opening Questions

Just as in other aspects of life, first impressions are important in survey work. The first few questions you ask will determine the tone for the survey, and can help put your respondent at ease. With that in mind, the opening few questions should, in general, be easy to answer. You might start with some simple descriptive questions that will get the respondent rolling. You should never begin your survey with sensitive or threatening questions.

Sensitive Questions

In much of our social research, we have to ask respondents about difficult or uncomfortable subjects. Before asking such questions, you should attempt to develop some trust or rapport with the respondent. Often, preceding the sensitive questions with some easier warm-up ones will help. But, you have to make sure that the sensitive material does not come up abruptly or appear unconnected with the rest of the survey. It is often helpful to have a transition sentence between sections of your instrument to give the respondent some idea of the kinds of questions that are coming.

A Checklist of Considerations

There are lots of conventions or rules-of-thumb in the survey design business. Here's a checklist of some of the most important items. You can use this checklist to review your instrument:

— start with easy, nonthreatening questions
— put more difficult, threatening questions near end
— never start a mail survey with an open-ended question
— for historical demographics, follow chronological order
— ask about one topic at a time
— when switching topics, use a transition
— reduce response set (the tendency of respondent to just keep checking the same response)
— for filter or contingency questions, make a flowchart

Golden Rule

You are imposing in the life of your respondent. You are asking for their time, their attention, their trust, and often, for personal information. Therefore, you should always keep in mind the "golden rule" of survey research:

To put this in more practical terms, you should keep the following in mind:

— Thank the respondent at the beginning for allowing you to conduct your study
— Keep your survey as short as possible—only include what is absolutely necessary
— Be sensitive to the needs of the respondent
— Be alert for any sign that the respondent is uncomfortable
— Thank the respondent at the end for participating
— Assure the respondent that you will send a copy of the final results

INTERVIEW METHOD

Interviews are among the most challenging and rewarding forms of measurement. They require a personal sensitivity and adaptability as well as the ability to stay within the bounds of the designed protocol.

Preparation of Interview

Role of the interviewer

The interviewer is really the "jack-of-all-trades" in survey research. The interviewer's role is complex and multifaceted. It includes the following tasks:

- *Locate and enlist cooperation of respondents:* The interviewer has to find the respondent. In door-to-door surveys, this means being able to locate specific addresses. Often, the interviewer has to work at the least desirable times (like immediately after dinner or on weekends) because that's when respondents are most readily available.
- *Motivate respondents to do good job:* If the interviewer does not take the work seriously, why would the respondent? The interviewer has to be motivated and has to be able to communicate that motivation to the respondent. Often, this means that the interviewer has to be convinced of the importance of the research.
- *Clarify any confusion/concerns:* Interviewers have to be able to think on their feet. Respondents may raise objections or concerns that were not anticipated. The interviewer has to be able to respond candidly and informatively.
- *Observe quality of responses:* Whether the interview is personal or over the phone, the interviewer is in the best position to judge the quality of the information that is being received. Even a verbatim transcript

will not adequately convey how seriously the respondent took the task, or any gestures or body language that were evident.

— *Conduct a good interview:* Last, and certainly not least, the interviewer has to conduct a good interview! Every interview has a life of its own. Some respondents are motivated and attentive, others are distracted or disinterested. The interviewer also has good or bad days. Assuring a consistently high-quality interview is a challenge that requires constant effort.

Training the Interviewers

One of the most important aspects of any interview study is the training of the interviewers themselves. In many ways the interviewers are your measures, and the quality of the results is totally in their hands. Even in small studies involving only a single researcher-interviewer, it is important to organise in detail and rehearse the interviewing process before beginning the formal study. Here are some of the major topics that should be included in interviewer training:

— *Describe the entire study:* Interviewers need to know more than simply how to conduct the interview itself. They should learn about the background for the study, previous work that has been done, and why the study is important.

— *State who is sponsor of research:* Interviewers need to know who they are working for. They—and their respondents—have a right to know not just what agency or company is conducting the research, but also, who is paying for the research.

— Teach enough about survey research: While you seldom have the time to teach a full course on survey research methods, the interviewers need to know enough that they respect the survey method and are motivated. Sometimes it may not be apparent why a question or set of questions was asked in a particular way. The interviewers will need to understand the rationale for how the instrument was constructed.

- *Explain the sampling logic and process:* Naive interviewers may not understand why sampling is so important. They may wonder why you go through all the difficulties of selecting the sample so carefully. You will have to explain that sampling is the basis for the conclusions that will be reached and for the degree to which your study will be useful.
- *Explain interviewer bias:* Interviewers need to know the many ways that they can inadvertently bias the results. And, they need to understand why it is important that they not bias the study. This is especially a problem when you are investigating political or moral issues on which people have strongly held convictions. While the interviewer may think they are doing good for society by slanting results in favour of what they believe, they need to recognise that doing so could jeopardise the entire study in the eyes of others.
- *"Walk through" the interview:* When you first introduce the interview, it's a good idea to walk through the entire protocol so the interviewers can get an idea of the various parts or phases and how they interrelate.
- *Explain respondent selection procedures, including*
  - *reading maps*: It's astonishing how many adults don't know how to follow directions on a map. In personal interviews, the interviewer may need to locate respondents who are spread over a wide geographic area. And, they often have to

navigate by night (respondents tend to be most available in evening hours) in neighbourhoods they're not familiar with. Teaching basic map reading skills and confirming that the interviewers can follow maps is essential.

- *identifying households:* In many studies it is impossible in advance to say whether every sample household meets the sampling requirements for the study. In your study, you may want to interview only people who live in single family homes. It may be impossible to distinguish townhouses and apartment buildings in your sampling frame. The interviewer must know how to identify the appropriate target household.
- *identify respondents:* Just as with households, many studies require respondents who meet specific criteria. For instance, your study may require that you speak with a male head-of-household between the ages of 30 and 40 who has children under 18 living in the same household. It may be impossible to obtain statistics in advance to target such respondents. The interviewer may have to ask a series of filtering questions before determining whether the respondent meets the sampling needs.
- *Rehearse interview*: You should probably have several rehearsal sessions with the interviewer team. You might even video-tape rehearsal interviews to discuss how the trainees responded in difficult situations. The interviewers should be very familiar with the entire interview before ever facing a respondent.
- *Explain supervision:* In most interview studies, the interviewers will work under the direction

of a supervisor. In some contexts, the supervisor may be a faculty advisor; in others, they may be the "boss." In order to assure the quality of the responses, the supervisor may have to observe a subsample of interviews, listen in on phone interviews, or conduct follow-up assessments of interviews with the respondents. This can be very threatening to the interviewers. You need to develop an atmosphere where everyone on the research team—interviewers and supervisors—feel like they're working together towards a common end.

- *Explain scheduling:* The interviewers have to understand the demands being made on their schedules and why these are important to the study. In some studies it will be imperative to conduct the entire set of interviews within a certain time period. In most studies, it's important to have the interviewers available when it's convenient for the respondents, not necessarily the interviewer.

Interviewer's Kit

It's important that interviewers have all of the materials they need to do a professional job. Usually, you will want to assemble an interviewer kit that can be easily carried and includes all of the important materials such as:

- a "professional-looking" 3-ring notebook (this might even have the logo of the company or organisation conducting the interviews)
- maps
- sufficient copies of the survey instrument
- official identification (preferable a picture ID)
- a cover letter from the Principal Investigator or Sponsor

— a phone number the respondent can call to verify the interviewer's authenticity

Beginning the Interview

So all the preparation is complete, the training done, the interviewers ready to proceed, their "kits" in hand. It's finally time to do an actual interview. Each interview is unique, like a small work of art (and sometimes the art may not be very good). Each interview has its own ebb and flow—its own pace. To the outsider, an interview looks like a fairly standard, simple, prosaic effort. But to the interviewer, it can be filled with special nuances and interpretations that aren't often immediately apparent.

Every interview includes some common components. There's the opening, where the interviewer gains entry and establishes the rapport and tone for what follows. There's the middle game, the heart of the process, that consists of the protocol of questions and the improvisations of the probe. And finally, there's the endgame, the wrap-up, where the interviewer and respondent establish a sense of closure. Whether it's a two-minute phone interview or a personal interview that spans hours, the interview is a bit of theatre, a mini-drama that involves real lives in real time.

Opening Remarks

In many ways, the interviewer has the same initial problem that a salesperson has. You have to get the respondent's attention initially for a long enough period that you can sell them on the idea of participating in the study. Many of the remarks here assume an interview that is being conducted at a respondent's residence. But the analogies to other interview contexts should be straightforward.

Gaining entry

The first thing the interviewer must do is gain entry. Several factors can enhance the prospects. Probably the most important factor is your initial appearance. The interviewer needs to dress professionally and in a manner that will be comfortable to the respondent. In some contexts a business suit and briefcase may be appropriate. In others, it may intimidate. The way the interviewer appears initially to the respondent has to communicate some simple messages—that you're trustworthy, honest, and non-threatening. Cultivating a manner of professional confidence, the sense that the respondent has nothing to worry about because you know what you're doing—is a difficult skill to teach and an indispensable skill for achieving initial entry.

Doorstep technique

You're standing on the doorstep and someone has opened the door, even if only halfway. You need to smile. You need to be brief. State why you are there and suggest what you would like the respondent to do. Don't ask—suggest what you want. Instead of saying "May I come in to do an interview?", you might try a more imperative approach like " I'd like to take a few minutes of your time to interview you for a very important study."

Introduction

If you've gotten this far without having the door slammed in your face, chances are you will be able to get an interview. Without waiting for the respondent to ask questions, you should move to introducing yourself. You should have this part of the process memorised so you can deliver the essential information in 20-30 seconds at most. State your name and the name of the organisation you represent. Show your identification badge and the letter that introduces you. You want to have as legitimate an appearance as possible. If you have a three-ring binder or clipboard with the logo of your organisation, you should have it out and visible. You should assume that the respondent will be interested in participating in your important study—assume that you will be doing an interview here.

Explaining the study

At this point, you've been invited to come in (After all, you're standing there in the cold, holding an assortment of materials, clearly displaying your credentials, and offering the respondent the chance to participate in an interview—to many respondents, it's a rare and exciting event. They hardly ever get asked their views about anything, and yet they know that important decisions are made all the time based on input from others.). Or, the respondent has continued to listen long enough that you need to move onto explaining the study. There are three rules to this critical explanation:

1) Keep it short;
2) Keep it short; and
3) Keep it short!

The respondent doesn't have to or want to know all of the neat nuances of this study, how it came about, how you convinced your thesis committee to buy into it, and so on. You should have a one or two sentence description of the study memorised. No big words. No jargon. No detail. There will be more than enough time for that later (and you should bring some written materials you can leave at the end for that purpose). This is the "25 words or less" description. What you should spend some time on is assuring the respondent that you are interviewing them confidentially, and that their participation is voluntary.

Asking the Questions

You've gotten in. The respondent has asked you to sit down and make yourself comfortable. It may be that the respondent was in the middle of doing something when you arrived and you may need to allow them a few minutes to finish the phone call or send the kids off to do homework. Now, you're ready to begin the interview itself.

Use questionnaire carefully, but informally

The questionnaire is your friend. It was developed with a lot of care and thoughtfulness. While you have to be ready to adapt to the needs of the setting, your first instinct should always be to trust the instrument that was designed. But you also need to establish a rapport with the respondent. If you have your face in the instrument and you read the questions, you'll appear unprofessional and disinterested. Even though you may be nervous, you need to recognise that your respondent is most likely even more nervous. If you memorise the first few questions, you can refer to the instrument only occasionally, using eye contact and a confident manner to set the tone for the interview and help the respondent get comfortable.

Ask questions exactly as written

Sometimes an interviewer will think that they could improve on the tone of a question by altering a few words to make it simpler or more "friendly." DON'T. You should ask the questions as they are on the instrument. If you had a problem with a question, the time to raise it was during the training and rehearsals, not during the actual interview. It is important that the interview be as standardised as possible across respondents. You may think the change you made was inconsequential when, in fact, it may change the entire meaning of the question or response.

Follow the order given

Once you know an interview well, you may see a respondent bring up a topic that you know will come up later in the interview. You may be tempted to jump to that section of the interview while you're on the topic. DON'T. You are more likely to lose your place. You may omit questions that build a foundation for later questions.

Ask every question

Sometimes you'll be tempted to omit a question because you thought you already heard what the respondent will say. Don't assume that. For example, let's say you were conducting an interview with college age women about the topic of date rape. In an earlier question, the respondent mentioned that she knew of a woman on her dormitory floor who had been raped on a date within the past year. A few questions later, you are supposed to ask "Do you know of anyone personally who was raped on a date?" You figure you already know that the answer is yes, so you decide to skip the question. Instead, you might say something like "I know you may have already mentioned this, but do you know of anyone personally who was raped on a date?" At this point, the respondent may say something like "Well, in addition to the woman who lived down the hall in my dorm, I know of a friend from high school who experienced date rape." If you hadn't asked the question, you would never have discovered this detail.

Don't finish sentences

I don't know about you, but I'm one of those people who just hates to be left hanging. I like to keep a conversation moving. Once I know where a sentence seems to be heading, I'm aching to get to the next sentence. I finish people's sentences all the time. If you're like me, you should practice the art of patience (and silence) before doing any interviewing. As you'll see below, silence is one of the most effective devices for encouraging a respondent to talk. If you finish their sentence for them, you imply that what they had to say is transparent or obvious, or that you don't want to give them the time to express themselves in their own language.

Obtaining Adequate Responses

OK, you've asked a question. The respondent gives a brief, cursory answer. How do you elicit a more thoughtful, thorough response? You probe.

Silent probe

The most effective way to encourage someone to elaborate is to do nothing at all—just pause and wait. This is referred to as the "silent" probe. It works (at least in certain cultures) because the respondent is uncomfortable with pauses or silence. It suggests to the respondent that you are waiting, listening for what they will say next.

Overt encouragement

At times, you can encourage the respondent directly. Try to do so in a way that does not imply approval or disapproval of what they said (that could bias their subsequent results). Overt encouragement could be as simple as saying "Uh-huh" or "OK" after the respondent completes a thought.

Elaboration

You can encourage more information by asking for elaboration. For instance, it is appropriate to ask questions like "Would you like to elaborate on that?" or "Is there anything else you would like to add?"

Ask for clarification

Sometimes, you can elicit greater detail by asking the respondent to clarify something that was said earlier. You might say, "A minute ago you were talking about the experience you had in high school. Could you tell me more about that?"

Repetition

This is the old psychotherapist trick. You say something without really saying anything new. For instance, the respondent just described a traumatic experience they had in childhood. You might say "What I'm hearing you say is that you found that experience very traumatic." Then, you should pause. The respondent is likely to say something like "Well, yes, and it affected the rest of my family as well. In fact, my younger sister..."

Recording the Response

Although we have the capability to record a respondent in audio and/or video, most interview methodologists don't think it's a good idea. Respondents are often uncomfortable when they know their remarks will be recorded word-for-word. They may strain to only say things in a socially acceptable way. Although you would get a more detailed and accurate record, it is likely to be distorted by the very process of obtaining it. This may be more of a problem in some situations than in others. It is increasingly common to be told that your conversation may be recorded during a phone interview. And most focus group methodologies use unobtrusive recording equipment to capture what's being said. But, in general, personal interviews are still best when recorded by the interviewer using pen and paper.

Record responses immediately

The interviewer should record responses as they are being stated. This conveys the idea that you are interested enough in what the respondent is saying to write it down. You don't have to write down every single word—you're not taking stenography. But you may want to record certain key phrases or quotes verbatim. You need to develop a system for distinguishing what the respondent says verbatim from what you are characterising (how about quotations, for instance!).

Include all probes

You need to indicate every single probe that you use. Develop a shorthand for different standard probes. Use a clear form for writing them in.

Use abbreviations where possible

Abbreviations will help you to capture more of the discussion. Develop a standardised system (e.g., R=respondent; DK=don't know). If you create an abbreviation on the fly, have a way of indicating its origin. For instance, if you decide to abbreviate Spouse with an 'S', you might make a notation in the right margin saying "S=Spouse."

Concluding the Interview

When you've gone through the entire interview, you need to bring the interview to closure. Some important things to remember:

- *Thank the respondent:* Don't forget to do this. Even if the respondent was troublesome or uninformative, it is important for you to be polite and thank them for their time.
- *Tell them when you expect to send results:* I hate it

when people conduct interviews and then don't send results and summaries to the people who they get the information from. You owe it to your respondent to show them what you learned. Now, they may not want your entire 300-page dissertation. It's common practice to prepare a short, readable, jargon-free summary of interviews that you can send to the respondents.

— *Don't be brusque or hasty:* Allow for a few minutes of winding down conversation. The respondent may want to know a little bit about you or how much you like doing this kind of work. They may be interested in how the results will be used. Use these kinds of interests as a way to wrap up the conversation. As you're putting away your materials and packing up to go, engage the respondent. You don't want the respondent to feel as though you completed the interview and then rushed out on them—they may wonder what they said that was wrong. On the other hand, you have to be careful here. Some respondents may want to keep on talking long after the interview is over. You have to find a way to politely cut off the conversation and make your exit.

— *Immediately after leaving—write down any notes about how the interview went:* Sometimes you will have observations about the interview that you didn't want to write down while you were with the respondent. You may have noticed them get upset at a question, or you may have detected hostility in a response. Immediately after the interview you should go over your notes and make any other comments and observations—but be sure to distinguish these from the notes made during the interview.

9

Scaling in Social Work Research

Most people don't even understand what scaling is. The basic idea of scaling is described in General Issues in Scaling, including the important distinction between a scale and a response format. Scales are generally divided into two broad categories: unidimensional and multidimensional. The unidimensional scaling methods were developed in the first half of the twentieth century and are generally named after their inventor. We'll look at three types of unidimensional scaling methods here:

- Thurstone or Equal-Appearing Interval Scaling
- Likert or "Summative" Scaling
- Guttman or "Cumulative" Scaling

In the late 1950s and early 1960s, measurement theorists developed more advanced techniques for creating multidimensional scales. Although these techniques are not considered here, you may want to look at the method of concept mapping that relies on that approach to see the power of these multivariate methods.

General Issues in Scaling

S.S. Stevens came up with what I think is the simplest and most straightforward definition of scaling. He said:

Scaling is the assignment of objects to numbers according to a rule.

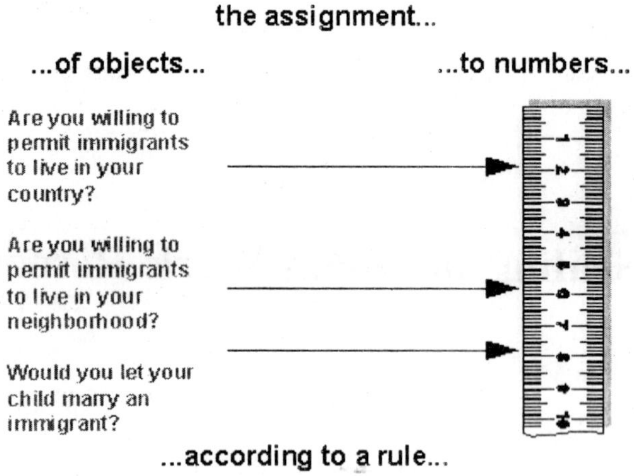

But what does that mean? In most scaling, the objects are text statements, usually statements of attitude or belief. The figure shows an example. There are three statements describing attitudes towards immigration. To scale these statements, we have to assign numbers to them. Usually, we would like the result to be on at least an interval scale as indicated by the ruler in the figure. And what does "according to a rule" mean? If you look at the statements, you can see that as you read down, the attitude towards immigration becomes more restrictive—if a person agrees with a statement on the list, it's likely that they will also agree with all of the statements higher on the list. In this case, the "rule" is a cumulative one. So what is scaling? It's how we get numbers that can be meaningfully assigned to objects—it's a set of procedures. We'll present several different approaches below.

People often confuse the idea of a scale and a response scale. A response scale is the way you collect responses from people on an instrument. You might use a dichotomous response scale like Agree/Disagree, True/

False, or Yes/No. Or, you might use an interval response scale like a 1-to-5 or 1-to-7 rating. But, if all you are doing is attaching a response scale to an object or statement, you can't call that scaling. As you will see, scaling involves procedures that you do independent of the respondent so that you can come up with a numerical value for the object. In true scaling research, you use a scaling procedure to develop your instrument (scale) and you also use a response scale to collect the responses from participants. But just assigning a 1-to-5 response scale for an item is not scaling! The differences are illustrated in the table below.

Scale	Response Scale
results from a process	is used to collect the response for an item
each item on scale has a scale value	item not associated with a scale value
refers to a set of items	used for a single item

Purposes of Scaling

Why do we do scaling? Why not just create text statements or questions and use response formats to collect the answers? First, sometimes we do scaling to test a hypothesis. We might want to know whether the construct or concept is a single dimensional or multidimensional one (more about dimensionality later). Sometimes, we do scaling as part of exploratory research. We want to know what dimensions underlie a set of ratings. For instance, if you create a set of questions, you can use scaling to determine how well they "hang together" and whether they measure one concept or multiple concepts.

But probably the most common reason for doing scaling is for scoring purposes. When a participant gives their responses to a set of items, we often would like to assign a single number that represents that's person's overall attitude or belief.

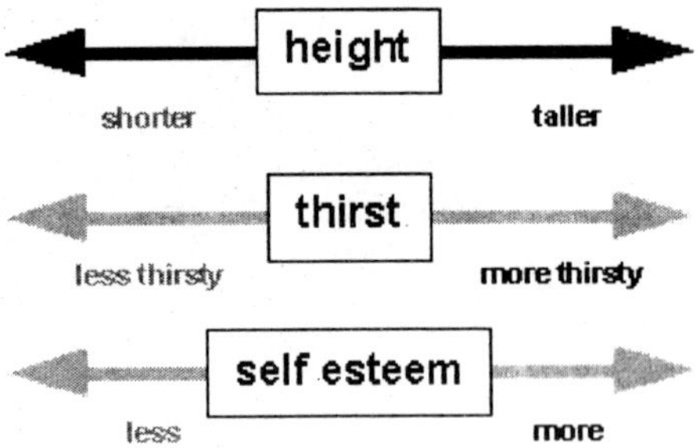

For the figure above, we would like to be able to give a single number that describes a person's attitudes towards immigration, for example.

Dimensionality

A scale can have any number of dimensions in it. Most scales that we develop have only a few dimensions. What's a dimension? Think of a dimension as a number line. If we want to measure a construct, we have to decide whether the construct can be measured well with one number line or whether it may need more. For instance, height is a concept that is unidimensional or one-dimensional. We can measure the concept of height very well with only a single number line (e.g., a ruler).

Weight is also unidimensional—we can measure it with a scale. Thirst might also bee considered a unidimensional concept—you are either more or less thirsty at any given time. It's easy to see that height and weight are unidimensional. But what about a concept like self esteem? If you think you can measure a person's self esteem well with a single ruler that goes from low to high, then you probably have a unidimensional construct.

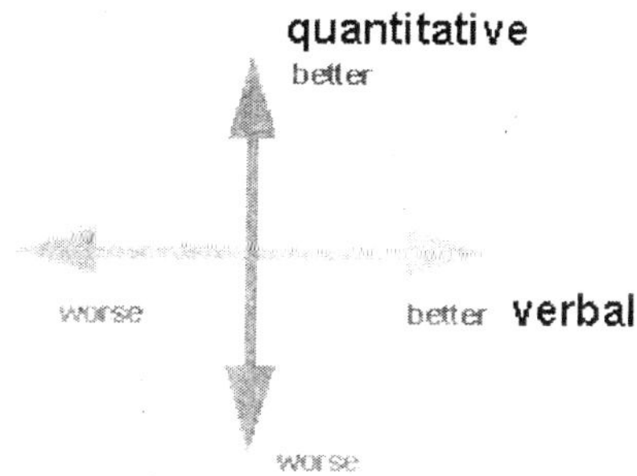

What would a two-dimensional concept be? Many models of intelligence or achievement postulate two major dimensions—mathematical and verbal ability. In this type of two-dimensional model, a person can be said to possess two types of achievement.

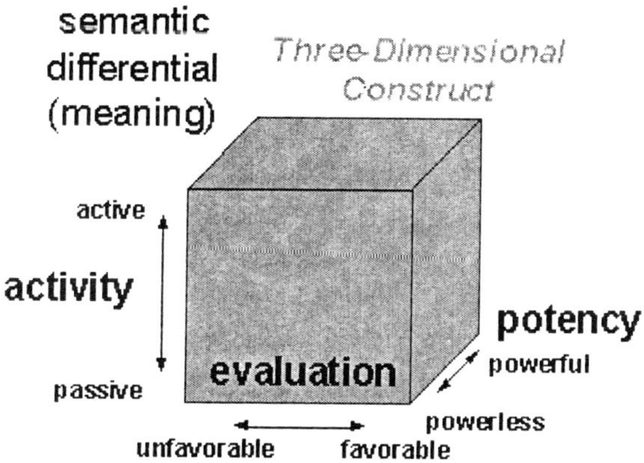

Some people will be high in verbal skills and lower in math. For others, it will be the reverse. But, if a concept is truly two-dimensional, it is not possible to depict a person's level on it using only a single number line. In other words, in order to describe achievement you would need to locate a person as a point in two dimensional (x,y) space.

OK, let's push this one step further: how about a three-dimensional concept? Psychologists who study the idea of meaning theorised that the meaning of a term could be well described in three dimensions. Put in other terms, any objects can be distinguished or differentiated from each other along three dimensions. They labelled these three dimensions activity, evaluation, and potency. They called this general theory of meaning the semantic differential. Their theory essentially states that you can rate any object along those three dimensions.

For instance, think of the idea of "ballet." If you like the ballet, you would probably rate it high on activity, favourable on evaluation, and powerful on potency. On the other hand, think about the concept of a "book" like a novel. You might rate it low on activity (it's passive), favourable on evaluation (assuming you like it), and about average on potency. Now, think of the idea of "going to the dentist." Most people would rate it low on activity (it's a passive activity), unfavourable on evaluation, and powerless on potency (there are few routine activities that make you feel as powerless!).

The theorists who came up with the idea of the semantic differential thought that the meaning of any concepts could be described well by rating the concept on these three dimensions. In other words, in order to describe the meaning of an object you have to locate it as a dot somewhere within the cube (three-dimensional space).

Unidimensional

What are the advantages of using a unidimensional model? Unidimensional concepts are generally easier to understand. You have either more or less of it, and that's all. You're either taller or shorter, heavier or lighter. It's also important to understand what a unidimensional scale is as a foundation for comprehending the more complex multidimensional concepts. But the best reason to use unidimensional scaling is because you believe the concept you are measuring really is unidimensional in reality.

As you've seen, many familiar concepts (height, weight, temperature) are actually unidimensional. But, if the concept you are studying is in fact multidimensional in nature, a unidimensional scale or number line won't describe it well. If you try to measure academic achievement on a single dimension, you would place every person on a single line ranging from low to high achievers. But how do you score someone who is a high math achiever and terrible verbally, or vice versa? A unidimensional scale can't capture that type of achievement.

There are three major types of unidimensional scaling methods. They are similar in that they each measure the concept of interest on a number line. But they differ considerably in how they arrive at scale values for different items. The three methods are Thurstone or Equal-Appearing Interval Scaling, Likert or "Summative" Scaling, and Guttman or "Cumulative" Scaling.

Define Thurstone Scaling

Thurstone was one of the first and most productive scaling theorists. He actually invented three different methods for developing a unidimensional scale: the method of equal-appearing intervals; the method of successive intervals; and, the method of paired comparisons. The three methods differed in how the scale values for items were constructed, but in all three cases, the resulting scale was rated the same way by respondents. To illustrate Thurstone's approach, I'll show you the easiest method of the three to implement, the method of equal-appearing intervals.

Method of Equal-Appearing Intervals

Developing the Focus. The Method of Equal-Appearing Intervals starts like almost every other scaling method—with a large set of statements. Oops! I did it again! You can't start with the set of statements—you have to first define the focus for the scale you're trying to develop. Let this be a warning to all of you: methodologists like me often start our descriptions with the first objective methodological step (in this case, developing a set of statements) and forget to mention critical foundational issues like the development of the focus for a project. So, let's try this again...

The Method of Equal-Appearing Intervals starts like almost every other scaling method—with the development of the focus for the scaling project. Because this is a unidimensional scaling method, we assume that the concept you are trying to scale is reasonably thought of as one-dimensional. The description of this concept should be as clear as possible so that the person(s) who are going to create the statements have a clear idea of what you are trying to measure. I like to state the focus for a scaling project in the form of a command—the command you will give to the people who will create the statements. For instance, you might start with the focus command:

Generate statements that describe specific attitudes that people might have towards persons with AIDS: You want to be sure that everyone who is generating statements has some idea of what you are after in this focus command. You especially want to be sure that technical language and acronyms are spelled out and understood. Generating Potential Scale Items. Now, you're ready to create statements. You want a large set of candidate statements (e.g., 80—100) because you are going to select your final scale items from this pool.

You also want to be sure that all of the statements are worded similarly—that they don't differ in grammar or structure. For instance, you might want them each to be worded as a statement which you cold agree or disagree with. You don't want some of them to be statements while others are questions. The other Thurstone scaling methods are similar to the Method of Equal-Appearing Intervals. All of them begin by focusing on a concept that is assumed to be unidimensional and involve generating a large set of potential scale items.

All of them result in a scale consisting of relatively few items which the respondent rates on Agree/Disagree basis. The major differences are in how the data from the judges is collected. For instance, the method of paired comparisons requires each judge to make a judgement about each pair of statements. With lots of statements, this can become very time consuming indeed. With 57 statements in the original set, there are 1,596 unique pairs of statements that would have to be compared! Clearly, the paired comparison method would be too time consuming when there are lots of statements initially. Thurstone methods illustrate well how a simple unidimensional scale might be constructed. There are other approaches, most notably Likert or Summative Scales and Guttman or Cumulative Scales.

Likert Scaling

Like Thurstone or Guttman Scaling, Likert Scaling is a unidimensional scaling method. Here, I'll explain the basic steps in developing a Likert or "Summative" scale. Defining the Focus. As in all scaling methods, the first step is to define what it is you are trying to measure. Because this is a unidimensional scaling method, it is assumed that the concept you want to measure is one-dimensional in nature. You might operationalise the definition as an instruction to the people who are going to create or generate the initial set of candidate items for your scale.

Generating the Items

Next, you have to create the set of potential scale items. These should be items that can be rated on a 1-to-5 or 1-to-7 Disagree-Agree response scale. Sometimes you can create the items by yourself based on your intimate understanding of the subject matter. But, more often than not, it's helpful to engage a number of people in the item creation step. For instance, you might use some form of brainstorming to create the items. It's desirable to have as large a set of potential items as possible at this stage, about 80-100 would be best.

Rating the Items

The next step is to have a group of judges rate the items. Usually you would use a 1-to-5 rating scale where:

1. = strongly unfavourable to the concept
2. = somewhat unfavourable to the concept
3. = undecided
4. = somewhat favourable to the concept
5. = strongly favourable to the concept

Notice that, as in other scaling methods, the judges are not telling you what they believe—they are judging how favourable each item is with respect to the construct of interest.

Selecting the Items

The next step is to compute the intercorrelations between all pairs of items, based on the ratings of the judges. In making judgements about which items to retain for the final scale there are several analyses you can do:

- *Throw out any items that have a low correlation with the total (summed) score across all items:* In most statistics packages it is relatively easy to compute this type of Item-Total correlation. First, you create a new variable which is the sum of all of the individual items for each respondent. Then, you include this variable in the correlation matrix computation (if you include it as the last variable in the list, the resulting Item-Total correlations will all be the last line of the correlation matrix and will be easy to spot). How low should the correlation be for you to throw out the item? There is no fixed rule here—you might eliminate all items with a correlation with the total score less that.6, for example.
- *For each item, get the average rating for the top quarter of judges and the bottom quarter:* Then, do a t-test of the differences between the mean value for the item for the top and bottom quarter judges. Higher t-values mean that there is a greater difference between the highest and lowest judges. In more practical terms, items with higher t-values are better discriminators, so you want to keep these items. In the end, you will have to use your judgement about which items are most sensibly retained. You want a relatively small number of items on your final scale (e.g., 10-15) and you want them to have high Item-Total correlations and high discrimination (e.g., high t-values).

Administering the Scale

You're now ready to use your Likert scale. Each respondent is asked to rate each item on some response scale. For instance, they could rate each item on a 1-to-5 response scale where:

1. = strongly disagree
2. = disagree

3. = undecided

4. = agree

5. = strongly agree

There are a variety possible response scales (1-to-7, 1-to-9, 0-to-4). All of these odd-numbered scales have a middle value is often labelled Neutral or Undecided. It is also possible to use a forced-choice response scale with an even number of responses and no middle neutral or undecided choice. In this situation, the respondent is forced to decide whether they lean more towards the agree or disagree end of the scale for each item.

The final score for the respondent on the scale is the sum of their ratings for all of the items (this is why this is sometimes called a "summated" scale). On some scales, you will have items that are reversed in meaning from the overall direction of the scale. These are called reversal items. You will need to reverse the response value for each of these items before summing for the total. That is, if the respondent gave a 1, you make it a 5; if they gave a 2 you make it a 4; 3 = 3; 4 = 2; and, 5 = 1.

Guttman Scaling

Guttman scaling is also sometimes known as cumulative scaling or scalogram analysis. The purpose of Guttman scaling is to establish a one-dimensional continuum for a concept you wish to measure. What does that mean? Essentially, we would like a set of items or statements so that a respondent who agrees with any specific question in the list will also agree with all previous questions. Put more formally, we would like to be able to predict item responses perfectly knowing only the total score for the respondent. For example, imagine a ten-item cumulative scale.

If the respondent scores a four, it should mean that he/she agreed with the first four statements. If the respondent scores an eight, it should mean they agreed with the first eight. The object is to find a set of items that perfectly matches this pattern. In practice, we would seldom expect to find this cumulative pattern perfectly. So, we use scalogram analysis to examine how closely a set of items corresponds with this idea of cumulativeness. Here, I'll explain how we develop a Guttman scale.

Define the Focus

As in all of the scaling methods. Let's imagine that you wish to develop a cumulative scale that measures U.S. citizen attitudes towards immigration. You would want to be sure to specify in your definition whether you are talking about any type of immigration (legal and illegal) from anywhere (Europe, Asia, Latin and South America, Africa).

Develop the Items

Next, as in all scaling methods, you would develop a large set of items that reflect the concept. You might do this yourself or you might engage a knowledgeable group to help. Let's say you came up with the following statements:

- I would permit a child of mine to marry an immigrant.
- I believe that this country should allow more immigrants in.
- I would be comfortable if a new immigrant moved next door to me.
- I would be comfortable with new immigrants moving into my community.
- It would be fine with me if new immigrants moved onto my block.

— I would be comfortable if my child dated a new immigrant.

Of course, we would want to come up with many more statements (about 80-100 would be desirable).

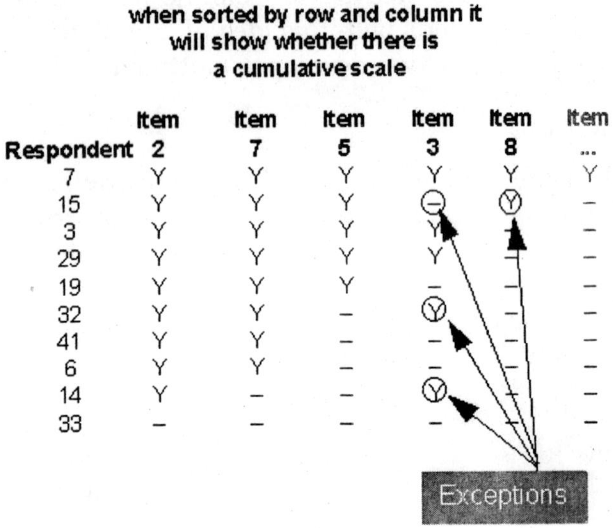

Rate the Items

Next, we would want to have a group of judges rate the statements or items in terms of how favourable they are to the concept of immigration. They would give a Yes if the item was favourable toward immigration and a No if it is not. Notice that we are not asking the judges whether they personally agree with the statement. Instead, we're asking them to make a judgment about how the statement is related to the construct of interest.

Develop the Cumulative Scale

The key to Guttman scaling is in the analysis. We construct a matrix or table that shows the responses of all the respondents on all of the items. We then sort this matrix so that respondents who agree with more statements are listed at the top and those agreeing with fewer are at the bottom. For respondents with the same number of agreements, we sort the statements from left to right from those that most agreed to those that fewest agreed to. We might get a table something like the figure. Notice that the scale is very nearly cumulative when you read from left to right across the columns (items). Specifically if someone agreed with Item 7, they always agreed with Item 2. And, if someone agreed with Item 5, they always agreed with Items 7 and 2. The matrix shows that the cumulativeness of the scale is not perfect, however. While in general, a person agreeing with Item 3 tended to also agree with 5, 7 and 2, there are several exceptions to that rule.

While we can examine the matrix if there are only a few items in it, if there are lots of items, we need to use a data analysis called scalogram analysis to determine the subsets of items from our pool that best approximate the cumulative property. There are several statistical techniques for examining the table to find a cumulative scale. Because there is seldom a perfectly cumulative scale we usually have to test how good it is. These statistics also estimate a scale score value for each item. This scale score is used in the final calculation of a respondent's score.

10

Ethics of Social Research

The Tuskegee Syphilis Study was conducted by the United States Public Health Service (USPHS) beginning in 1932. The study examined untreated cases of latent syphilis in human subjects to determine the "natural course" of the disease. Three hundred and ninety nine black males from Tuskegee, Alabama, who already had late-stage syphilis, were recruited for this study along with a matched sample of 201 noninfected males. The subjects were not asked to provide their informed consent in order to participate in this project.

Those infected with syphilis in the early 1930s were given the standard treatment at that time, which consisted of administering heavy metals. However, those men participating in the study were, not treated. In fact, the doctor in charge of the study noted "everyone is agreed that the proper procedure is the continuance of the observation of the negro men used in the study with the idea of eventually bringing them to autopsy".

However, when antibiotics became available in the 1940s and it was evident that this treatment would improve a patient's chances for recovery, antibiotic treatment was withheld from the infected subjects, even though the researchers knew that if left untreated the disease would definitely progress to increased disability and eventually early death. According to some reports, "on several occasions, the USPHS actually sought to prevent treatment".

The experiment lasted over four decades, and it was not until 1972, in large part prompted by exposure from the national media, that government officials finally ended the experiment. By that time "74 of the test subjects were still alive; at least 28, but perhaps more than 100 had died directly from advanced syphilis". There was a government investigation of the entire project launched in mid 1972, and a review panel "found the study 'ethically unjustified' and argued that penicillin should have been provided to the men".

Ethical Lessons Learned from the Tuskegee Biomedical Experimenta

At no time in the course of this project were subjects asked to give their consent to participate in the study. They were not told about the particulars of what the study would entail. In fact, those who participated did not volunteer for the project! Instead, they were deceived into thinking that "they were getting free treatment from government doctors for a serious disease. It was never explained that the survey was designed to detect syphilis... Subjects were never told they had syphilis, the course of the disease, or the treatment, which consisted of spinal taps".

In his book Bad Blood: The Tuskegee Syphilis Experience, author James Jones notes that the subjects in the Tuskegee experiment had a blind trust in the medical community. As one subject from the experiment notes:

> We trusted them because of what we thought they could do for us, for our physical condition... We were just going along with the nurse. I thought [the doctors] was doing me good.

There is also a question of whether or not the researchers took advantage of a vulnerable population whom they knew did not have the resources to afford medical treatment or the education to question their medical expertise. In addition, the researchers' stereotypical racist attitudes about black males made it easier to justify their decision to not provide them with treatment:

> The rationale was that the conditions existed "naturally" and that the men would not have been treated anyway, according to the premise that shaped the study-that African Americans, being promiscuous and lustful, would not seek or continue treatment. Poor decisions on the part of the researchers, influenced by bigotry, allowed this to happen.

But this kind of research is simply unacceptable. It demonstrates how racism can lead to inhuman treatment of human subjects. It is argued that the effects of this experiment have to some extent created a long-lasting impact on the black American community, casting a "long shadow on the contemporary relationship between African Americans and the biomedical community".

Centrality of Ethics in the Research Process

Ethical discussions usually remain detached or marginalised from discussions of research projects. In fact, some researchers consider this aspect of research an afterthought. Yet, the moral integrity of the researcher is a critically important aspect of insuring that the research process and a researcher's findings are "trustworthy" and valid. The term ethics derives from the Greek word ethos which means character. To engage with the ethical dimension of your research requires asking yourself several important questions:

– What moral principles guide your research?

- How do ethical issues enter into your selection of a research problem?
- How do ethical issues affect how you conduct your research-the design of your study, your sampling procedure, etc.?
- What responsibility do you have toward your research subjects? For example, do you have their informed consent to participate in your project? What ethical issues/dilemmas might come into play in deciding what research findings you publish? Will your research directly benefit those who participated in the study?

A consideration of ethics needs to be a critical part of the substructure of the research process from the initial conception of your problem to the interpretation and publishing of the research findings.

History of Research Ethics

Formal consideration of the rights of research subjects grew out of the revelations of the terrible atrocities that were performed in the guise of scientific research on Jews and other racial and ethnic minority groups in Nazi concentration camps during World War II. One result of the revelations of these appalling medical experiments perpetrated in the name of science resulted in the creation, in 1949, of the Nuremberg Code, a code of ethics, which starts off with the stipulation that all research participation must be voluntary.

Other codes of ethics soon followed, including the Declaration of Helsinki. This code was specifically developed "in part as an alternative to the Nuremberg Code, which dealt exclusively with nontherapeutic [research promising no direct benefit to the subject] research". This code protects research subjects in both therapeutic and nontherapeutic contexts. The Declaration of Helsinki notes several central procedures that should be applied in biomedical research:

> Every biomedical research project involving human subjects should be preceded by careful assessment of predictable risks in comparison with foreseeable benefits to the subject or to others... The right of the research subject to safeguard his or her integrity must always be respected. Every precaution should be taken to respect the privacy of the subject and to minimise the impact of the study on the subject's physical and mental integrity and on the personality of the subject.

The Council for International Organisation of Medical Sciences (CIOMS) was also created for those researching in developing nations. Throughout the history of scientific research, ethical issues have captured the attention of scientists and the media alike. While extreme cases of unethical behaviour are the exception not the rule in the scientific community, an accounting of these projects can provide important lessons for understanding what can happen when the ethical dimension of research is not considered holistically within the research process.

Guidlines and Laws Governing the Research Process

Unfortunately, when the Tuskegee experiment began, there was no institutional review board (IRB) to oversee the goals of the project. It was not until the mid 1960s that the federal government began the process of developing a set of "official rules" governing the treatment of research, partly in response to such medical abuses as the Tuskegee experiment and others, which ultimately led to the passage by Congress in 1974 of the National Research Act. This act set up an Office for the Protection of Research Risks (OPRR) and was housed in the National Institutes of Health (NIH).

The act called for the establishment of a "Commission on Protection of Human Subjects of Biomedical and Behavioural Research". These ethical principles were released by the Commission in 1978 in a report known as the "Belmont Report," which was later revised to incorporate additional protections for young children who participate in the research process. In 1991, these revised guidelines, known as the Common Rule, received widespread adoption by federal agencies.

The Common Rule mandated, among other things, that any institution receiving federal funds for research must establish an institutional review committee. These committees, known as Institutional Review Boards (IRBs), have the job of watching over all research proposals that involve working with human subjects and animals. Universities and colleges, for example, that receive federal funding for research on human subjects are required by federal law to have review boards or forfeit their federal funding.

IRBs are responsible for carrying out U.S. government regulations for human research. They must determine whether the benefits of a study outweigh its risks; that consent procedures have been carefully carried out and that no one group of individuals has been unfairly treated or left out of the potential positive outcomes of a given study. This is, of course, important in a hierarchically structured society where we can't simply assume racism, sexism, homophobia, and classism won't make their way into research.

Certain types of research, for example, educational research dealing with "instructional strategies," may have an "exempt status" and a full review by an IRB may not be required. It is noteworthy that, over the course of more than four decades, even after the USPHS had finally set up a Code of Research Ethics for the treatment of research subjects, the Tuskegee experiment was still allowed to continue. This raises questions about how effective and accountable research projects are to IRBs as well as about the effectiveness of the range of professional ethics codes that are part of most professional associations and currently serve as guidelines for conducting research.

Protecting Human Subjects in Research Studies

It has been over thirty years since the government issued its regulations for protecting human subjects in research studies receiving federal funding, yet there continue to be cases involving human subjects that have resulted in harm and death. As one researcher notes: "The history of research involving human subjects has been described by ethicists as one of 'progress propelled by scandal". Concerning the current scandals in the field of biomedical research, Alvino says:

> ... the highly publicised death of Jesse Gelsinger, a research subject who died as a result of his participation in a gene therapy trial at the University of Pennsylvania, aroused significant media attention and public concern regarding the safety of clinical trials. His story is far from unique... Medical research suffered another blow... when it was discovered that researchers and pharmaceutical companies involved in research at Cornell and Tufts had failed to notify the National Institutes of Health that six gene therapy research subjects had died during experiments over a nineteen-month period.

At the centre of many of the debates regarding the protection of human subjects is the question of whether informed consent procedures are sufficient to protect human subjects, and the ability of IRBs to oversee the research process in their home institutions. Why didn't the IRBs report the deaths of research subjects to the federal agencies involved in funding these projects? Were the research subjects given proper information regarding the side effects of the study?

In the case of Jesse Gelsinger, he was an 18-year-old college student at the time he participated in the University of Pennsylvania study in 1999. An investigation of his death showed that (1) he in fact was not a good candidate for the study in the first place, and (2) he was not provided with adequate information concerning the extreme adverse side effects that other participants in the study had experienced. Jesse's father notes: "[I]t looked safe. It was presented as being safe... I was misled". This has too often been the case.

Professional associations such as the American Educational Research Association (AERA), the American Sociological Association (ASA), and the American Psychological Association (APA) also outline general ethical guidelines for their members. Each of these associations has a website that discusses a range of specific ethical concerns in each of these professions.

The American Psychological Association's website for example, outlines specific ethical categories of conduct, from general principles of professional conduct that deal with issues such as integrity and justice to more practice-specific concerns such as privacy and confidentiality of patients and research subjects. There are also ethical guidelines on record keeping and fees as well as ethical guidance on issues that may come up in a therapeutic situation, such as those especially pertaining to sexual intimacy with clients and therapy with former sexual partners. There are also guidelines for resolving ethical issues, such as how to handle complaints and discrimination.

Thus far we have been focusing on biomedical research. To what extent do the ethical issues in the sciences carry over into the behavioural and social sciences? Researchers conducting biomedical studies often present a "protocol" that outlines the specific steps they will follow in conducting research on human subjects. Qualitative research is, by its very nature, open to discovery and change in research goals.

It may be nearly impossible for the qualitative researcher to account for all of the happenings in the research setting, and it may be hard to go back and forth to a Human Subjects Committee (like an IRB) for approval each time a project takes an unexpected turn. Adler and Adler argue that obtaining informed consent hits those researchers practicing participant observation the hardest:

> Participant observation has a fuzziness about what is research and what is not, as ethnographers are observers of everyday life and may be generating insights and gathering data from people in all kinds of situations (a waitress at a restaurant, a fellow passenger on an airplane, a person whose child is the same age as one's own). They may not know in advance what information will drift their way and that may prove explicitly useful, either currently or in the future.

In addition, there is often a very personal engagement with research subjects that is often not found to the same extent in biomedical research, raising even more prominently the possibility of undue power, influence, and authority being wielded in the research process. There are some "classic" examples of extreme violations of ethics in the annals of behavioural and social scientific research as well.

Perhaps one of the most egregious comes from a 1963 research project on "obedience to authority," conducted by psychologist Stanley Milgram. Milgram wanted to understand the conditions under which individuals obey authority figures. His research protocol called for deceiving volunteer subjects into thinking they were involved in an experiment on the impact of punishment on memory. Volunteers first read a series of word associations to the individuals (confederates) under a variety of experimental conditions:

(1) where they could not see or hear the confederate;

(2) they could hear the confederate protest but not see the confederate;

(3) they could hear and see the confederate;

(4) same conditions as (3) except the subject was required to place the confederate's hand on a shock plate.

If confederates were unable to repeat the words, volunteers were asked to administer an "electric shock" to them, increasing the voltage for each wrong answer in order to enhance learning. Subjects had a fake voltage meter in front of them with readings "from slight to severe shock," with a sign warning of the danger in using the equipment posted next to the meter. Some subjects protested upon hearing confederates complain about pain and other medical problems.

Even though some volunteers wanted to quit the experiment, the researcher in charge insisted that they continue, saying that he (the researcher) would take responsibility. Some subjects, however, did not protest and even went on to administer what they considered the "highest," most lethal, shock to a confederate, even when they had received no feedback that the person was even alive. Stanley Milgram's experiment deceived his volunteer subjects and failed to obtain their informed consent.

The protocol of this experiment did not allow subjects to quit even when some protested and asked that it be stopped. In addition, some subjects experienced psychological distress knowing they actually could administer what would be considered a lethal shock to another human being.

Ethical Dilemma of Covert Research

Some researchers argue that their research must be conducted in a "covert" manner in order to obtain the information they need to understand certain social phenomena. For example, researchers have gone undercover to study such underground cultures as the drug culture and used deception in order to find out about the inner workings of the social life of drug dealers and drug takers, often observing individuals engaging in illegal activities and sometimes finding themselves asked to engage in these same activities.

There would be no point in asking for the informed consent of the members of this closed society, since they would most likely not want their organisation studied. Williams, who did participant observation on a subculture of cocaine users and dealers in the after-hours clubs in an inner city, notes the following concerning his undercover activities:

> I was in a Brooklyn club where I was already conspicuous as a nonuser of cocaine. It seems that I was also oversealous. In the sense that I was staring too much and asking too many questions. One of the club's owners came over to me and said "Listen, my man, if you're undercover, I got people that'll take care of that." I was not sure whether he meant force or bribery, but in any case I stopped going to that club... As a researcher, I knew what data I needed: information on cocaine users and the associated nightlife, street myths about use... But as most researchers know there is a quid pro quo in every research situation... I was asked to do a variety of favours, such as lending money and finding social workers... On many occasions I was asked to engage in illegal acts.... This and similar requests put me in an awkward position.

- Is it ethical to go undercover?
- Is it ethical to engage in illegal activities under the guise of research?

One can imagine those social scientists studying deviant behaviours, such as life in the underground drug trafficking world, and how difficult it might be to obtain the informed consent of everyone involved in order to study the inner workings of the illicit drug trade.

- What does the researcher do when he or she confronts information or situations where individuals are observed to engage in major violations of the law?
- Is the researcher ethically obligated to report such activity?
- What about the risks the researcher is taking in terms of his or her own life if they do so?

Deception in research doesn't have to occur by going "undercover" in carrying out research projects. The Milgram experiment was a study in deception. From the start, Milgram did not truthfully explain the nature of the experiment, and he deceived subjects into thinking they were in fact applying electrical shocks to another human being.

Some qualitative social science research methods, like fieldwork, also require some type of deception between the researcher and the researched. Sociologist Herbert Gans, conducting fieldwork in Park Forest, a suburb near Chicago, in Boston's West End, and in Levittown, a New Jersey suburb, relates his personal reflections on the anxiety he experienced in what he finds is "the deception inherent in participant observation":

Once the fieldworker has gained entry, people tend to forget he is there and let down their guard, but he does not; however much he seems to participate, he is really there to observe and even to watch what happens when people let down their guard. He is involved in personal situations in which he is, emotionally speaking, always taking and never giving, for he is there to learn and, thus, to take from the people he studies, whereas they are always giving information, and are rarely being given anything.

Of course they derive some satisfaction from being studied, but when they ask the participant observer to give-for example, help or advice-he must usually refuse in order to maintain his neutrality. Moreover, even though he seems to give of himself when he participates, he is not really doing so and, thus, deceives the people he studies. He pretends to participate emotionally when he does not; he observes even when he does not appear to be doing so and like the formal interviewer, he asks questions with covert purposes of which his respondents are likely to be unaware. In short, psychologically, the participant observer is acting dishonestly; he is deceiving people about his feelings and in observing when they do not know it, he is spying on them.

Herbert Gans represents a particular point of view on the role of the researcher as participant in the fieldwork experience. The idea that the researcher should remain neutral and "detached" from the research subject tells us that he or she aspires to the goal of "objectivity" in the research process. This objectivity then is enhanced by deception. Yet, as we have seen, this frame on the research process is one of many paradigms one can bring to the fieldwork experience.

There are those who believe the researcher does not need to maintain distance between the researcher and the researched. Ann Oakley, in fact, critiques this model of neutrality and instead argues for bridging this divide through empathy and affinity. Other ethnographers feel that this form of closeness between researcher and researched also has its problems and that one can become too close to respondents. This in turn can create a series of conflicts and deceptions. Ethnographer Judith Stacey comments:

> ... the irony I now perceive is that the ethnographic method exposes subjects to far greater danger and exploitation than do more positivist, abstract, and "masculinist" research methods. And the greater the intimacy -the greater the apparent mutuality of the researcher/researched relationship-the greater is the danger.

Stacey notes that the further involved she became with her respondents the further exposed she became to situations within the field that left her open to the possibility of manipulating and betraying her respondents. So we can see that issues of disclosure and trust are actually very complex.

Some might argue that a certain amount of "strategic" deception is needed when researchers are especially interested in "studying up". The study of elites is not a common practice within the social sciences. The elite and semi-elite population hold key positions within society, yet their activities and power remain invisible to the average citizen. Elites often protect their privacy through a myriad of self-imposed barriers, ranging from unlisted phones and email accounts to the hiring of staff to screen their calls and contacts and security personnel to prevent unwanted contact with those outside their elite culture.

Adler and Adler note that current IRB and professional associations who fear lawsuits have developed codes of ethics that now ban all aspects of covert research, using the argument that it is almost impossible to obtain informed consent. In addition, these boards cannot protect the researcher from revealing the identity of their respondents if they are asked to do so by officials investigating their research findings. Adler and Adler note:

> Clearly, if we are being told that we cannot protect our own subjects from official investigation short of our or

> their going to jail, which not everyone is willing to do, some changes are necessary. Is the new system the best way? If you fundamentally shut down research there is no risk to subjects because researchers will not know anything.

Johnson and Altheide reflect on professional ethics, given their 65 years of combined experience as university scholars. They note the lack of legal protection of social scientists regarding the confidentiality of their sources as a "political" and not a moral issue:

> In the United States, the first amendment of the constitution protects journalists by guaranteeing free speech and a free press. Social scientists lack such protection regarding confidentiality of sources, however, and we surmise that this is best seen as a political, rather than a moral one. If social scientists had such protection, we speculate that we might be addressing a different set of ethical issues-perhaps ones such as how social scientists abuse their constitutional protection.

Adler and Adler argue that ethics boards have overstepped their function, which has resulted in the unanticipated outcome of favouring the dominant classes over the weaker: "Powerful, elite groups can now better hide their mechanisms of control, while weak and powerless groups have lost the ability to tell their stories from their own perspective".

These researchers lament the fact that covert research, such as that done by Erving Goffman in his classic work, Asylums, which provides readers with a bird's eye view of the treatment of the mentally ill by those who care for them, and that carried out by Gary Marx on the activities of control agencies such as the police, will no longer be possible under the new ethics guidelines.

Haggerty has identified what he terms an "ethics creep" that has taken over social science research "in the name of ethics." He defines this term as follows: "This is characterised by a dual process whereby the regulatory system is expanding outward to incorporate a host of new activities and institutions, while at the same time intensifying the regulation of activities deemed to fall within its gambit"

Conflicts of Interest in the Research Process

Academics are under financial pressures from their universities to obtain grants for research. More and more of these grants are coming from commercial institutions such as drug companies:

> The sharp increase in privately funded research has created an atmosphere that breeds conflicts arising from compelling financial incentives. These conflicts may arise from researchers' financial relationships with companies whose products they are studying, whether the research is sponsored by the government or by the company itself.

In some cases, universities are becoming enmeshed with industrial research interests. Angell points out the problem of academic medicine being "for sale." She notes:

> Academic medical institutions are... increasingly beholden to industry... Some academic institutions have entered into partnerships with drug companies to set up research centres and teaching programmes in which students and faculty members essentially carry out industry research. Both sides see great benefit in this arrangement. For financially struggling medical centres, it means cash. For the companies that make the drugs and devices, it means access to research talent, as well as affiliation with a prestigious brand.

It is possible that in some cases members of a university's own IRB boards can have a vested interest in the very studies they have oversight on. Alvino notes:

> Although IRB members are supposedly foreclosed from participating in review of any project or study in which

> they have a conflicting interest... there is no way to ensure that the research facility or individual researchers are not operating under such conflicts.

An article in the L.A. Times cited a Yale University study which remarked that "one quarter of the biomedical researchers at universities had commercial ties serious enough to raise questions of financial conflict".

- What are the ethical implications of accepting funding for research?
- How can academics and IRBs work together most effectively?
- How can funding sources, such as the National Science Foundation (NSF) or The National Institute of Mental Health (NIMH), help alleviate the tensions between funding research and ethics?

Ethical Dilemma

Bell and Nutt talk about their "divided loyalties" in terms of how their professional and occupational commitments pull them in many different directions, creating ethical dilemmas arising from the multiple roles they bring to a research setting. Linda Nutt describes how her professional role as a social work practitioner who is "bound by general social work codes of practice" conflicted with her role as researcher:

> As she was leaving the home of a new carer following the research interview Linda Nutt noticed an unambiguously sexually explicit picture in the hallway. For most researchers this would not be an issue; art is a matter of personal taste. But Linda Nutt wasn't just a researcher she was also a practitioner. Frequently when children are placed in foster homes little is know about their life experiences so new carers are instructed to assume that all children have been sexually abused unless specifically told otherwise... There is a statutory responsibility to disregard confidentiality where children are at risk. Nonetheless,

> because she wanted to keep the roles clear and separate-to act as a researcher (and be in receipt of information) and not as an employee... (who could give then information), Linda Nutt chose not to tackle this issue with these new careers but spent several days considering this ethical dilemma. In the end the social worker practitioner identity overcame that of the researcher identity and Linda Nutt informed the local authority of her unease regarding the picture and its potential impact upon the foster children.

Some researchers employ research techniques that raise ethical issues regarding how human subjects are treated. Homan notes what he calls the "softening up" techniques to get at more personal information from respondents who may be unwilling to talk:

> The insidiousness of softening-up techniques is demonstrated by some impertinent questions reserved for the latter and more compliant stages of the interviews and questionnaires: having scrupulously sought and obtained a general consent from respondents and their parents.

By its very nature, qualitative research often requires emotional engagement with those with whom we build knowledge. Jean Duncombe and Julie Jessop discuss how some researchers can lack sympathy for their respondents and "fake" their interest and concern for those they research. Jean Duncombe describes how she wound up treating some of her respondents in a research project she was conducting:

> ... we found it more difficult to achieve rapport where we did not spontaneously feel empathy with our interviewees. For example in an early study of Youth Training Schemes (YTS), Jean felt she established a "genuine," if shallow rapport with the YTS trainees and with the more conscientious employers who took training seriously, because she was "on their side." But with the more exploitative employers and trainers (who provided neither jobs nor training), she knew she was faking rapport to "betray" them into revealing their double standards, and sometimes whilst smiling at them she almost smiled to herself, thinking: "What a revealing quote"... Julie felt

> uncomfortable and personally compromised when she found that, in order to obtain a "good" interview, it seemed necessary to smile, nod and appear to collude with views she strongly opposed.

Researchers are human just like everyone else. Accordingly, we all bring our own likes, dislikes, emotions, values, and motivations to our research projects. It is unrealistic to expect that you will always like those you research, or that you will always naturally feel 100% engaged. This being said, bear in mind that it is you, the researcher, who has initiated this process and involved others. Consider this carefully as you contemplate your ethical obligations to your research participants, but as you think through these issues, do so with your own "humanness" in mind-be realistic and fair to all involved.

Solution for Ethical Abuses in Research

A major principle underlying many of the ethical policies which have historically grown up around the issue of how to treat research subjects has been the use of "informed consent," the right of subjects to decide anonymously whether they will be involved in a research endeavour. Some ethicists question the extent to which informed consent has lived up to the promise of anonymity for research subjects.

Research has pointed out that subjects do not always understand the medical aspects of the clinical project they are participating in, and some do not even know that they may in fact be participating in a research trial. As we have seen earlier in this chapter, there are many instances in which there is failure to fully disclose to research subjects the full extent of the risks and benefits of participating in a study, and this has led to some disastrous research outcomes for some of those who participated in clinical trials and biomedical research.

There is, then, a practice and a reality to providing informed consent. There exists a wide variation in how well researchers carry out the policy of informed consent in their ongoing research projects. For example, we present two types of letters on informed consent a researcher might write to parents regarding their child's participation in a research project on body image. Wee observe that "Letter A" contains a much more detailed account of the research problem, including several research goals and an explanation of how the research will be carried out.

It may not always be in the interest of the researcher to be forthcoming regarding full disclosure. Some researchers may even go out of their way to explain the research project as a "cover story," and this may be built into the original design of the research project:

> The selection or invention of details to constitute the cover story and convince intended respondents is an element in the design of a research project. That requires skills of persuasion. Investigators develop a sense of what details allay fears and what prompt suspicions. As in other types of negotiation, such as bargaining over salaries, the initiating party uses a gambit declaring a position which it may concede and which supposes an opposition of interests between the negotiating parties. The investigator will reveal further information if required but in many cases subjects will not be briefed to ask pertinent questions and the project will move on quickly from negotiation to interview.

If respondents initially refuse to participate in a research project, rather than accepting the right of the researched to act autonomously, this is often viewed as a failure on the part of the researcher, and there is a tendency of the researcher to break down "the defenses of respondents" through a variety of means, from group pressure to exploitation of friendships. To this issue, Homan says:

> In various ways research projects trade upon a relationship with agencies in power or authority. Sutherland was able to research the secretive and exclusive Rom community, which was normally hostile to representatives of the world outside it by exploiting her role as teacher of its children.

There are even times when following ethical guidelines may not always be in the best interests of your research respondents. Baez points out the ethical conundrum he experienced in maintaining the confidentiality of his respondents.

Baez interviewed 16 minority faculty members regarding their personal experiences with the tenure and promotion process at one private university. He notes that maintaining confidentially can be a double-edged sword. Keeping the interviews confidential, especially for untenured faculty, allowed him to obtain candid data regarding racism and sexism within this university.

On the other hand, confidentiality prevented him from reporting "... serious contradictions within an institution that, through institutional documents and public comments by key administrators, purported to be supportive of racial and cultural diversity... I could not do so without feeling that I would be identifying my respondents to others in the institution". Bear in mind that you often don't know what your research will teach you, and it can be very difficult not to try and effect social change in some situations.

Patton notes that respondents are now maintaining their right to "tell their stories" without hiding their identities, especially when they see the project as an opportunity to gain empowerment through telling their stories and perhaps becoming a catalyst for social change. Patton suggests a number of important ethical dilemmas that flow from this new viewpoint on confidentiality:

- Should the researcher "impose confidentiality against the wishes of those involved?"
- Are human subjects committees "patronising and disempowering" if they turn down those respondents who wish to reveal their identities?
- Does the research subject make the choice independent of others in their social context? What about the privacy of significant others in their lives, such as children, spouse, and extended family members?

There is a great deal we can learn from this example. Specifically, Maddison shows how ethical practice is an ongoing consideration. Moreover, ethical issues and informed consent provide the researcher with an opportunity to learn about themselves and develop as researchers-ethics are a doorway to reflexivity.

Practice of Ehtics in Social Research

Ethics exist within a social context. The ethical dilemmas we discussed in this chapter serve to remind us of the importance of including an ethical perspective in the very foundation of our research project. Ethical rules cannot possibly apply to all events that can happen in a given project. Rubin and Rubin note that ethical guidelines do not begin to cover all of the ethical dilemmas you may face in the practice of social research:

> You cannot achieve ethical research by following a set of preestablished procedures that will always be correct. Yet, the requirement to behave ethically is just as strong in qualitative interviewing as in other types of research on humans-maybe even stronger. You must build ethical routines into your work. You should carefully study codes of ethics and cases of unethical behaviour to sensitise yourself to situations in which ethical commitments become particularly salient. Throughout your research, keep thinking and judging what are your ethical obligations.

A useful distinction we might keep in mind here is the difference between what Homan terms ethical codes and ethical values. Agreeing to comply with ethical codes as outlined in an informed consent proposal does not absolve the researcher from adhering to the underlying ethical values contained in these codes, yet very often "they invite observance in the letter rather than in the principle". Homan reminds us that the danger is that many researchers think their moral obligation begins and ends with the signing of the letter of consent. In some cases an informed consent letter is seen as one protecting the researcher more than the researched. One anthropologist notes:

> I fear that informed consent, when mechanically applied using a form or some verbal formula, becomes more of a protection for the researcher than the researched. Informed consent obtained in this way is unilateral rather than bilateral and protects the researcher against charges from participants that they did not understand fully the intent or outcome of the research. Ethics does not exist in a vacuum. As King, Henderson, and Stein note:
>
> ... the ethics of human subjects research may be universal but is at the same time deeply particularised, so that what autonomy or informed consent or confidentiality or even benefit and harm means depends on the circumstances. The circumstances do not determine whether any of these "Western" moral concepts applies, but how.

Emergent Issues in Ehtics Research

King, Henderson, and Stein's observations on ethical behaviour point to a shift in thinking about how ethics is incorporated into the research process. They discuss a paradigmatic shift in thinking of ethics as a based on moral principles largely independent of specific circumstances, to one based on a view of ethics embedded in contextual relationships.

A principalist might be concerned about the inherent "relativistic" point of view contained within a relational ethics perspective, while a relationalist might charge a principalist with "moral imperalism, paternalism and absolutism. Ethics viewed through each of these paradigmatic lenses asks different types of questions, and it weighs in differently on what priorities should be stressed in a discussion of the ethics of human subjects research. Up to now, a principalist paradigm has guided the development of the ethics guidelines for IRBs and professional associations.

11

Community in Social Work Research

New research techniques and tools have produced important advances in community studies in other fields, but these developments have not sufficiently influenced social work practice research to date. With respect to social work practice in community, the question of building knowledge for control is complicated by the fact that community may be the agent of change, the target of change or the context for change. Figure 1 presents a diagram of the various points of entry for research on community change.

The central concept of community can be studied as a dependent variable, independent variable, mediating variable or a moderator variable. There are numerous examples of features that have been put forward as essential for healthy, strong, sustainable or effective communities such as: social capital, including bridging and bonding capital, community capacity including leadership, governance, and organisation, collective efficacy, sense of community, social control, neighbouring, amenities and resources, institutional strength, inter-organisational relations, civic participation, and stressors and violence, among others. Any and all of these may be the targets of social intervention. Practice research needs to demonstrate how interventions with communities can produce changes in these important attributes and processes. Moreover, knowledge for control requires evidence regarding the mediating processes that enable this change so that the exact methods can be specified and replicated.

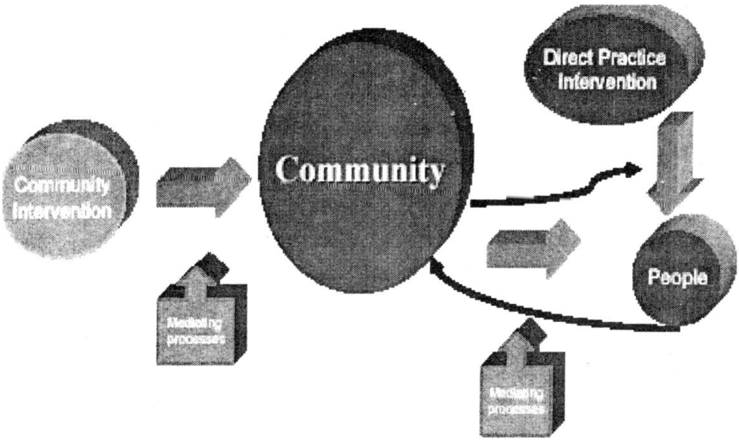

Figure 1: Model of Community in Social Work Research

On the right hand side of Figure 1, the symbol labelled "people" indicates that it is also important to demonstrate how community change affects the well being of individuals. In fact, the ultimate goal of many community change efforts is to promote the health of the population, achieve employment gains, or reduce problem behaviours or conditions. It is also vital, as shown in Figure 1, for research to demonstrate the mediating processes through which community impacts upon individual outcomes. Knowledge about the workings of mediating processes in communities will allow interventions to be crafted toward greater precision and effectiveness. Community conditions or processes may also moderate the impact of direct practice interventions, and research is needed on the circumstances under which interventions are more or less effective and why.

Moreover, it is incumbent upon social work research to uncover deleterious community conditions that may appear to be individual risk factors. Interventions targeted at individuals' risk factors may be less effective and efficient than those that eliminate or reduce the root causes in the context. Finally, as symbolised by the reverse arrow in Figure 1, community change may be produced as a result of individual change, especially in the aggregate. For example, movement of residents in and out of communities may change the attributes and processes of the community, especially when that movement produces shifts in the age, socio-economic status, ethnicity, culture or other demographics which may in turn transform norms, expectations, relationships and practices within the community. Furthermore, individual residents acting on their own or as groups are powerful sources of community change.

The above model reveals the pivotal place of community in social work practice research. However, research to inform this practice has been hampered by a number of practical, technical and theoretical problems including:

— *Defining community boundaries.* The specification of community as a unit for study and action has been unclear and problematic. Researchers have either been vague about the units that constitute the community or have relied on arbitrary statistical definitions that do not represent the importance of place. These ambiguities have undermined the authenticity and statistical power of community studies and biased downward the estimates of community effects.

- *Specifying interventions.* Community interventions have been difficult to specify so that they can be replicated. The fact that community interventions have many actors, complex objectives and generally call for community participation has made them challenging to document. They tend not to comply with the prevailing template for researchable interventions that can be captured in protocols and evaluated for fidelity and compliance.
- *Developing community measures.* Research cannot move forward without careful measurement, but methods to measure community attributes and processes have not been given as much attention as the psychometrics of individual behaviour. Community researchers have tended to invent their own tools, making studies difficult to compare and build into an evidence base.
- *Applying multi-level statistical models.* Statistical models have not always been optimal for community level data. Until recently, statistical tests ofcommunity effects were either reduced to models of individual perception, or ecological correlations among aggregated counts or rates. Neither type of model addressed the vital questions about places as ecological units, residents as individuals and the relationships among them. Moreover, one-level models often violated statistical assumptions.
- *Establishing the counterfactual.* Community research has also foundered on the grounds of causal attribution. Many of the principles of solid research design that support causal inference have been impractical in the study of community interventions. The gold standard of randomised experiments was virtually untried until recently, and the search for community effects has been mired in concern about selection bias and simultaneity.

— *Assessing spatial and geographic processes.* Community research has been essentially divorced from where the communities are actually located, and what processes within or between them are fostered or impeded by space or distance. Geography has been virtually unaccounted for in most studies of community intervention and influences of proximity and distance have been overlooked.

Community and Neighbourhood Boundaries

Research on communities must establish boundaries for the purposes of data collection and analysis. A common method of doing this when multiple communities are being studied has been to rely on statistical definitions of community, such as census tracts, school zones or zip codes. A limitation is that these units are unlikely to be identical to the spaces that influence residents' lives or the actual boundaries for action. Alternatively, in case studies of single communities, there is often a lack of specification of community boundaries at all. Actions and actors are described, but it is not clear where they are located and how they relate to the entire area that is the community. The problem is that if the community unit is not correctly specified for the purposes of the research, the effects will be obscured. Generally speaking, much research on community has used areas that are too large to be effective in terms of social intervention or effects. Community effects are thus biased downward. Moreover, it is important for researchers to realise that the community boundaries may change over time, or vary depending upon the purpose to which they are being put.

Advances in Geographic Information Systems (GIS) technology make it possible to use information from community members or other stakeholders to construct the boundaries of communities and to collect and analyse data that fit these socially constructed spaces. For example, Coulton, Korbin, Chan and Su asked random samples of neighbourhood residents to draw out their personal views of their neighbourhoods on GIS generated maps. These maps were digitised and analysed using spatial statistics.

Another approach to defining communities uses GIS to identify patterns of intersecting, pedestrian streets that are deemed to be areas of social interaction. Grannis has demonstrated that these natural breaks represent boundaries across which social interaction diminishes. He has used GIS to examine hypotheses about space and social organisation and to define community units for further analysis.

The use of GIS tools to uncover socially meaningful boundaries can make community research more authentic, accurate and replicable. By examining resident perceptions, street intersections and geographic attributes, the research can link social, economic and behavioural data to community areas that are defined from varying perspectives. Such community units can also be linked to specific interventions, projects or actions that test hypotheses about practice. Vague or inappropriate boundaries undermine the power and generalisability of community research, but GIS combined with local perceptions can be used to derive clear and relevant definitions of community units.

Fidelity and Replicability of Community Interventions

Community interventions pose challenges for research because they are often implemented through a participatory action process that is incremental and emergent by design. Numerous individuals and groups may be involved in a complex and diverse set of activities, which are difficult to document and measure in sufficient detail so that they can be replicated. Although these initiatives are typically guided by a set of principles and draw upon practice experience, the tacit knowledge of members of the community isoften an important ingredient in shaping the intervention. Converting these sources of knowledge to an intervention plan that can be studied has proven daunting.

Several approaches to evaluation have the potential to improve the precision with which community interventions are described and documented while holding fast to the principles of participation. In this technique, all participants in an initiative are solicited for their implicit theory about how they expect to achieve the desired improvements in their community. The change process is laid out in a series of early, interim and ultimate outcomes along with benchmarks that can be measured or observed. Often the benchmarks are ones that the community can be involved in monitoring. The so-called outcomes are changes that in other parlance may have been labeled inputs or process measures, but they are occurrences that are believed to be necessary and sufficient to push the process of change in the desired direction.

The logic model and the measures that are made on each outcome can provide the type of detailed documentation needed for specifying replicable interventions. Similarly, some approaches to empowerment evaluation involve careful documentation and monitoring of the intervention. Community participants are empowered through contributing to specification of objectives and monitoring results. The internet can facilitate the collection of comparable documentation data from multiple participants and communities by imposing a uniform web-based template of definitions and criteria.

These illustrations point to the feasibility of studying comparable interventions in multiple communities while at the same time maintaining the principle of community participation. These methods should allow the field to move away from its reliance on the single and unique case study approach. Although case studies are rich in context and texture, they are limited in the degree to which they build the evidence base for practice. To cumulate knowledge, the field must be able to compare across replications and to determine when interventions are alike or different in important ways.

Measuring Community Attributes and Processes

Too much of the research on local communities relies upon compositional measures from the decennial census. Numerous studies claim to test community effects even though the only aspects of the community represented in the empirical models are socio-economic status and demographic make up of the population. However, to study community interventions, an array of social, economic and physical structures and processes need to be measured. Social work researchers must invest considerably more resources toward developing relevant and accurate measures of those aspects of community that are relevant to practice.

Few currently available instruments capture what makes a community a desirable place toraise children, or enables an area to demand its fair share of services, maintain responsive institutions, cope with threats or disasters or other such signs of a vital and healthy place. The term "ecometrics", coined by Raudenbush and Sampson conveys the importance of raising community measurement to greater prominence. It needs to garner the same attention that has led to the large inventory of well-validated instruments pertaining to individual behaviours, abilities, attitudes and so forth, which rest on a strong foundation of psychometric theory and methods. The measures available for communities are not nearly as well established.

There are several promising developments, though, regarding measurement of communities. These advances rest on the recognition that community concepts cannot be treated simply as if they were perceptions or characteristics of individuals. For example, it is now understood that special attention needs to be given to establishing the reliability of aggregate measures. When community residents respond to a survey and their responses are combined to represent an attribute of their community, the reliability of the individual measure is a necessary but not sufficient condition for a reliable measure of the aggregate. In other words, it cannot be assumed that some concept that is well measured on individuals can be summed or averaged to capture that aspect of community. More appropriately, generalisability theory can be applied to calculate the reliability of these aggregate measures. Reliability coefficients can also be modeled equivalently through hierarchical linear modelling. The aggregate reliability coefficient is defined as:

$$\sum[\tau_{00}/(\tau_{00}+\sigma^2/n_j)]/J$$

where J is the number of neighbourhoods, n is the sample size in each neighbourhood, τ_{00} is the proportion of variance between neighbourhoods and σ^2 is the proportion of variance within neighbourhoods.

The reliability of the aggregate measure depends upon the number of respondents per community, the number of communities and the ratio of variation between and within communities. All else being equal, when community members have a fairly high level of agreement about an aspect of their community on which they are reporting, there will be high reliability for the measure. When there is poor agreement, it raises the possibility that there is really more than one community being represented in the community sample, or that the items are ambiguous enough that they mean different things to different people. Generalisability coefficients confirmed the reliability of many of these scales when 20 respondents per block group were used as informants. Several scales though, showed poor aggregate reliability, even though they were based on scales that displayed good internal consistency reliability at the individual level.

Contributing significantly to the advancement of community measurement theory and practice has been the massive undertaking of the Project on Human Development in Chicago Neighbourhoods. This project has invested heavily in the development and validation of novel methods and instruments in over 380 neighbourhood units. The multidisciplinary team of researchers has developed techniques of systematic social observation of block faces, using innovative approaches to videotaping and coding that are designed to capture mediating processes. These have been combined with a wealth of geocoded administrative records and with resident surveys that can be used to expand upon and cross-validate the observations. Observational tools and administrative records have been used effectively for neighbourhood research in other cities, but never on such a grand scale.

Finally, there are several collaborative efforts to make data and measures that are suitable for community analysis more readily accessible. The National Neighbourhood Indicators Partnership (NNIP) is comprised of organisations in 35 cities that compile measures of community well being. NNIP promotes systematic and ongoing collection, dissemination and use of indicators that go beyond the usual census based measures and incorporate observation, administrative records, surveys and other data sources.

The member cities all make the indicators available for use in social change efforts and support the fundamental democratisation of information. Another effort to advance the field of community measurement is an online catalogue provided by the Aspen Institute's Roundtable on Comprehensive Community Initiatives for Families and Children. This searchable inventory of measurement tools grew out of the groups' multi-year investigation into the challenges of evaluating community initiatives. The group concluded that investment in measurement was a necessary first step toward building creditable knowledge about how interventions could change communities.

Multi-level Designs and Analysis

In crafting social interventions, it is vital to be able to distinguish between the influence of individual, micro-level attributes or risk factors and effects of the larger context. It would be ideal to know what individuals bring with them regardless of context, which outcomes are mainly a consequence of the context to which individuals are exposed, and which are due to particular combinations of individual attributes and context. In fact, achieving a beneficial articulation between persons and their environments has been an organising principle of social work. The availability of tools and methods for multilevel analysis should facilitate research on community context and practice.

Without the benefit of multilevel modelling, research on contextual effects has often been reduced to the individual level in which community is represented by linking Neighbourhood variables to person level data. Actual places are not specified, but represented as variables that describe selected characteristics of persons' census tracts, such as the poverty rate or presence of middle class neighbours. Such models are problematic on both substantive and statistical grounds. When community is specified as a set of individual-level variables, the place is not represented as an organic whole. Moreover, to the degree that persons are nested within communities, statistical assumptions of independence are violated. Alternatively, there are also limitations of models that aggregate individual outcomes to the census tract or other geographic unit in order to study community effects. Although suggestive, ecological correlations cannot reliably demonstrate the influence of communities on individual residents.

Multilevel modelling, now readily available, allows researchers to examine individual and community influences within one model. These statistical models are based on nested research designs. In the case of community research, residents (level 1) are nested within communities (level 2). Communities might also be nested within larger regions such as labour markets or states (level 3). The total variance in any outcome can be decomposed into each level, for example, the variance that is between communities and within communities.

At each level, a structural model can be specified and estimated. The structural models may include variables at both levels that are hypothesized to influence the dependent variable. If communities are assigned to treatment and control conditions, the impact can be modeled at level 2 as a dummy variable. If individuals have been assigned to treatment and control conditions, this could be modeled as a dummy variable at level one. Cross-level interaction effects are tested to determine whether the effects of variables at one level are moderated by variables at the other level. It is also possible to explore whether factors have cross-level indirect effects, which may be an important research question when community intervention is hypothesized to benefit individuals through changing personal risk and protective factors.

Hierarchical Linear Modelling and its associated software (HLM) is the most commonly used approach to multi-level modelling in social work research. In the basic two level model, the statistical model for level 1 is:

$$Y_{ij} = \beta_{oj} + \sum_{q=1}^{Q} \beta_{qj} X_{qij} + r_{ij} \qquad r_{ij} \sim N(0, \sigma^2)$$

where Y_{ij} is the outcome variable for respondent i in community j. β_{oj} is the mean of the outcome score for community j. X represents the individual level predictors numbered from 1 to Q. Thus, X_{qij} is the qth predictor, for respondent i in community j; β_{oj} is the slope of the qth predictor for site j. The r_{ij} are errors assumed to be independent and normally distributed with a mean of 0 and variance, σ^2.

Level 2 attempts to explain the between-community variation using a set of explanatory factors that are community specific characteristics and processes according to the following statistical model:

$$\beta_{hj} = \gamma_{h0} + \sum_{k=1}^{K} \gamma_{hk} W_{kj} + U_{hj} \qquad U_{hj} \sim N(0, \tau_{hh})$$

where h is numbered from 0 to Q communities, W represents community factors numbered from 1 to K, and γ_{hk} represents the effect of the kth community factor on the hth parameter from level 1. In addition, there is an unexplained random effect (U_{hj}) for each (j^{th}) community.

The complete specification yields a large and complex parameterisation including full cross-level interactions. The equations can be estimated simultaneously using restricted maximum likelihood by the HLM software.

Multilevel modelling is an effective tool to identify the degree to which community features may promote or undermine the effectiveness of social work interventions with individuals and families. This is vitally important, because interventions are often piloted without regard to where the subjects live. Yet, when successful interventions are taken to scale, they are going to be implemented in many communities that have particular features and circumstance. Community variation is onepossible reason why interventions that work in carefully controlled demonstrations may be more or less effective elsewhere.

Establishing the Counterfactual

Although the question of what is solid evidence for practice is open to debate, many proponents see the randomised experiment as the gold standard. The reason is that a plausible counterfactual is needed to prove a causal relationship. The counterfactual represents what would have happened to the community or its residents in the absence of a condition or intervention of interest. A control group, created through random assignment, is arguably the best approximation of this counterfactual. Studies of community interventions or effects have faced serious challenges in the establishment of the counterfactual. Case studies and observational designs have predominated, leading to the inability to rule out selection bias, reverse causality and other threats to causal inference. However, the ideal of random assignment is very difficult to achieve when communities are the unit of analysis, either as independent or dependent variable. There are several recent developments, though, that hold promise in this regard.

Although it has been problematical to imagine the random assignment of communities to treatment and control groups, it is not unrealistic to think of community comparisons as the basis for a counterfactual. There is growing interest in whether the effectiveness of interventions can be studied using a combination of matched comparison communities and time series designs. By combining these techniques, communities that receive an intervention can be matched with comparison communities and tracked on important outcomes over a baseline period. Following the onset of the intervention, they can be tracked on these same outcomes going forward. An interrupted time series is a stronger design than a simple pre-post test, because the baseline trend can serve as a counterfactual. By adding the matched comparison communities, the trend is not only observed in intervention communities but can be compared with trends in communities without the intervention, eliminating history and maturation as alternative explanations for change.

In the community development field this approach has been tested using a difference in differences model. In three cities, trends in housing values were compared for intervention neighbourhoods and other neighbourhoods that were not part of the community development initiative. Moreover, the matching was more effective when the baseline trend was stable enough to be clearly ascertained.

A similar approach has been successfully applied in the Jobs Plus initiative. Treatment and comparison public housing communities were compared on employment outcomes before and after an intervention that was geared toward transforming the community into one that supported employment. Time series analysis was made possible by measuring employment trends in these communities for multiple years prior to and after the intervention to determine the difference in differences. The comparison of each community with itself over time through repeated measures presumably controls for unobserved, non-time varying, differences in the treatment and comparison communities other than the intervention, thus presenting a more compelling counter factual than case studies or simple pre and post test designs. These methods do require archival data to create a historical time series that is long enough to identify the trend, and thus may not be feasible in some instances.

A refinement of the matching algorithm involves matching multiple block groups or census tracts pulled from an entire region or large city to the block groups or census tracts that are within a target area for intervention. Working with small block groups rather than trying to find a match for the entire target area provides more degrees of freedom and many more units to pick from. The matches can be made using a number of characteristics, based either on direct matching or a propensity score model. Thus, the design does not require finding matches for target areas as a whole, which might be quite infeasible, but for the many (smaller) units of geography within an intervention community.

Researchers at MDRC have explored applying this technique to the evaluation design for Neighbourhood employment interventions. Their findings suggest the need for having sufficient numbers of Neighbourhood units to work with and an extensive array of characteristics on which to make a solid match. Without that, it is possible that heterogeneity (or error variance) within the treatment and comparison communities may overwhelm the power of any practical comparisons. The feasibility of using matched comparison communities to evaluate interventions to promote maternal and infant health has also been explored with some success in Baltimore.

Another type of community research question that calls for design improvements pertains to studies in which community is the independent variable. These investigations attempt to determine the effects of communities on the people who live there or to isolatethe moderating effect of community on the success of interventions. These types of studies usually suffer from internal validity problems due to selection; that is, persons either choose or are constrained to be in particular communities. This leads to an undeterminable correlation between unmeasured personal characteristics and Neighbourhood characteristics. Another internal validity problem of these studies is simultaneity or reverse causality; this occurs if individuals choose communities as a result of their outcomes, such as when employment success allows individuals to choose better neighbourhoods rather than vice versa. Up until recently, the only tools researchers had at their disposal to correct for these biases were imperfect statistical adjustments.

Moving to Opportunity (MTO) is an important experiment that tackles these problems head on and establishes the feasibility of random assignment as a tool in community research. The MTO experiment was implemented in five cities to determine whether public housing residents' outcomes could be improved by enabling them to move to low-poverty census tracts. Volunteers were randomly assigned to one of 3 conditions: an MTO treatment group that was offered housing vouchers and mobility counselling to relocate to neighbourhoods with poverty rates of less than 10 percent; a Section 8 comparison group that was offered rent vouchers to move anywhere outside of public housing; or a control group that was not offered vouchers at all. Findings are beginning to emerge in several early reports for each city and in a combined interim five-year impact evaluation. Overall, the results are mixed. The treatment group shows large improvements in sense of safety and Neighbourhood satisfaction, but there are only modest impacts on some aspects of health and behaviour, and no effects on parental employment and income.

A concern is that these early results may lead to the conclusion that neighbourhoods have little effect on outcomes for families and children. However, MTO also illustrates that random assignment of individuals to a mobility experiment has some limits in terms of what can be learned about community effects. Most importantly, since the treatment group was assigned to a low poverty rate, not particular places, the study does not actually permit a test of the effects of other community characteristics and social processes.

Moreover, even the influence of the poverty factor is diminished because many families in the treatment group actually did not relocate to a low poverty Neighbourhood, as the lease up rate was only about 50 percent. Additionally, the new neighbourhoods, although lower in poverty, tended to still be in the central city rather than the suburbs, implying a restriction of range on Neighbourhood quality. Nevertheless, the massive and successfully implemented MTO experiment represents a very important advancement in rigorous designs to study residential relocation and the effects of Neighbourhood poverty.

Spatial Patterns and Processes

Most social work practice research to date treats place-based communities as independent entities without explicit investigation into the role that proximity or contiguity plays. Within communities, conditions are assumed to be constant, rather than varying depending on geographic location. However, social processes and services within and between communities may be affected by geography, and interventions may be moreor less effective depending on their spatial properties. Recently available spatial statistics and GIS tools can be used to investigate these patterns.

A potentially useful application in social work research is the determination of the role that distance plays in the success of community interventions or well being of community residents. Using GIS tools, the distances among residents or local organisations or between communities and other places can be calculated and used in various analyses of social interventions or outcomes. For example, several studies have used GIS tools to develop measures of the geographic distance to regional job openings in inner city neighbourhoods. These indexes of job access have been shown to potentially moderate the success of welfare to work programmes. Also, distance matrixes to services have been used to construct service access measures. Using this technique, researchers have shown that living in a

Neighbourhood with better geographic access enables individuals to more appropriately utilise services. Geographically specific business information also has been used to demonstrate that access to amenities such as shopping and personal services is restricted in African-American neighbourhoods, possibly to their detriment. Improved geographic access to jobs, services and amenities could serve as important outcome measures for community interventions.

Spatial statistics can also be used to investigate the degree to which phenomenon are spatially clustered.

Local area auto correlation statistics (Moran's I) and contiguity analyses can reveal whether particular events are spatially related. For example, Sabol and Mikelbank examined spatial clustering and interaction of sellers and purchasers of illegal drugs across neighbourhoods in Cleveland.They used GIS software and SpaceStat to calculate local auto correlation statistics and weighted measures of contiguity between the residential Neighbourhood and the Neighbourhood in which the drug offense was committed.

Another way that the spatial locations of communities can be taken into account in research is through testing spatially lagged models. These models also use spatial contiguity matrices and weights developed from GIS data and have been applied in studies of violence in Chicago neighbourhoods. Determining the pattern of geographic dispersion of an outcome is another application of GIS that might be fruitful for studying community interventions. For example, Neighbourhood employment interventions have worked to link inner city communities with suburban employers so that Neighbourhood residents can travel there to get better jobs. An outcome such as employment dispersion can be quantified using a spatial descriptive statistic, the standard deviation ellipse (SDE).

12

Trends in Social Work Education and Research

Historically, programmes of social work education are informed by humanistic values and encompass knowledge of social problems, an understanding of individuals and their environment in interaction, and method of intervention into social and human difficulties. At the same time, structure of social work within the educational system and the length of training vary considerably from country to country. There is no serious international standards' setting for social work education, programmes, educators and students around the world.

Education programmes exist at differing levels of education and for differing periods of time. There are no worldwide data on the number and qualifications of teachers of social work, the number and characteristics of social work students, variations in curricula and type of practicum. North American and European models have had a major influence on social work educational programmes in most parts of the world, especially developing countries.

Still, the amount of western influence on social work education in developing countries is an issue that continues to be discussed. The programmes in practice in Europe and North America have influenced the implementation of social work education programmes. In recent years this influence has had a big part in the acceptance of the generalist approach. It is very important that social work education programmes must be planned in accordance with the social structure and the development process of the society.

Social Services in Turkey

Turkey occupies a surface area of 774 815km^2. About three percent of the total area lies in the South-eastern Europe and the remainder in South-western Asia. Turkey has borders with Greece, Bulgaria, Syria, Iraq, Iran, Georgia, Armenia and Nahcivan (Azerbaijan). In 1972, Turkey's population was 13.6 million according to the census, which was conducted four years after the establishment of the Republic. According to the results of the census conducted in 2000 the population of Turkey was 67- 8 million. The latest estimate of population growth rate was 15.1 per thousand for the 1990 - 2000 period. According to the projections, the population of Turkey was expected to reach 76 million by the year 2000.

As a result of the high fertility and growth rates of the recent past Turkey has a young population structure. Recent decades have witnessed dramatic declines especially in fertility rates. The total fertility rate was around 5 children per woman in the early 1970ies; it declined down to 2.57 children in 2000. The latest estimates put life expectancy at 66 years for males and 71 for females and infant mortality rate 41.9 per thousand.

The population of Turkey has undergone and intensive processes of urbanisation, especially from the 1950ies onwards. According to the 2000 population census 65 percent of the population in Turkey are living in urban settlements (province and district centres). The rate of urbanisation has been 59.2 during the last ten years period. The process of urbanisation has inevitably caused problems in the provision of services and emergence of large areas of squatter housing in unplanned cities.

Social services have a deep rooted past in the history of Turkey. The Ottomans religious foundations and some professional organisations performed active work in this field. After the Republic was founded in 1923, the public institutions conducted social services. Turkey is in a period of rapid social and economic development, and social welfare services provided to socially or economically disadvantaged citizens. Social services legal definition is as follows:

> "Social services are systematic, programmed services with the objective of helping individuals of families deprived through no fault of their own but on account of their environment to avoid and solve material, moral and social inadequacies and social problems and to improve their living conditions".

It is important to add that social services are not only concerned with the removal of problems caused by the poverty. In Turkey, as elsewhere, there are people who, although not actually poor, but are unable to enjoy the living standards of society and need to adopt. The mentally and physically handicapped, the aged and lonely people etc. The concept of social services in Turkey includes both types of services:

- People whose living conditions are bad due to their economic situation
- People who don't face economic problems but who are in need of professional services.

Social Services and child Protection Agency is responsible from these services by the law 2828. The General Directorate of Social Services and Child Protection Agency is the largest social assistance organisation of

Turkey, with its provisional directorates in 80 provinces. It provides support to children, adolescents, aged and disabled persons and families. In this context, service is provided through 295 establishments including the children homes, educational homes, homes for elderly, rehabilitation centres, day care centres, women's guesthouses, youth homes, foster families, adoption services and assistance in cash and kind to needy persons and families.

The Social Services and Child Protection Agency owned social services has the power and authority to give guidance to other public centre organisations and to assist privately owned social services institutions in their work, to issue permits and conduct supervisory services. The agency gives special importance and support to the cooperation with non-governmental organisation (NGOs) and local administrations, includes various regulations aiming at the community participation. In the administrative structure of Turkey, governors are top officials responsible for the administration in the provinces. Governors are in charge of the implementation and coordination of the social services in the provinces.

In this field, there are Social Services Advisory Councils in the provinces whose members include mayor, representatives from people and public institutions and the governors head these councils. Additionally there are non-governmental organisations like associations and foundations under all social service institutions. There are on going protocol between non-governmental organisations and the agency with the purpose of using resources more effectively and encouraging the volunteering people and organisations into the social services.

The major organisations of the social security today are,

- The social insurance organisation
- The social security fund for civil servants
- The social security agency for artisans and self employed.

Social Work Education in Turkey

Following the second world war the United nations were effective in increasing social services especially in the developing countries and founding schools to educate social workers. In the country the United Nations gave much support to the founding and development of the social services schools. Following the arrival of the United Nations Social Welfare Consultants, meetings were held with representatives of relevant ministries, public, private and volunteer organisations in 1957. The social services institute was founded in Turkey in 1959.

In the regulations of the social services institutes responsibilities were stated as follows:

- Reasons for poverty must be investigated and necessary social work must be determined.
- To avoid social deviations the necessary steps must be investigated.
- Normal and handicapped children must be protected and educated during the pre school years as well as during the school years.
- Children, teenagers and adults must be socially and economically supported.
- Work programmes of the rehabilitation organisations must be assisted.
- From the social services points of view cooperation must be established between all relevant organisations.

- Coordination must be established among volunteer organisations.
- Statistical data must be collated on social services.
- The aims of social services must be introduced to the public.
- To be able to realise all these aims schools in the form of a "Social Service Academy" need to be established to train the future social workers. It was decided to give four years training to the high school (lise) graduates. The first Academy was founded in 1961 with the objectives:
    1. To train social workers to have knowledge of social work methods and professional skills.
    2. To train social workers who are able to participate effectively in social policy and planning at various levels and who are able to plan, organise, administer, practice and undertake research in a variety of social welfare settings.

These trained social workers were to work in various situations:

- The welfare of the family and children,
- Medical and psychiatric health,
- Welfare of the poor,
- Geriatric and underprivileged care,
- Rehabilitation of physically disabled,
- Counselling for criminal offenders,
- Arranging spare time activities, social services and community organisations for students, to improve the life style of the community.

During the foundation process of the "Social Services Schools" the first group of Turkish teachers were joined by American social work educators with grants from the United Nations and the U.S. Fullbright programme. Members of the "Dutch technical Aid Commission" and the "Fullbright Commission" were also welcomed as advisors and teachers. Organisations such as Cento, the "Dutch Technical Aid Commission" gave and Fullbright Commission gave Turkish trainees grants to study social work abroad, on their return they took responsibility for training of others.

The first students of the Turkish "Social Services Academy" graduated in 1965. According to the research assistant regulations; examinations were held and those successful were admitted to be trained as lecturers. At this time as the "Social Service Academy" was not attached to a university, the students who wanted to do postgraduate studies had to obtain their degrees either from the relevant Departments of the universities here or from the universities abroad. The academy was joined to the Hacettepe University in 1983 and acquired the name "School of Social work", and then the students were able to do master and doctorate studies on social work here in Turkey.

Until 2002 Hacettepe University, School of Social work continued to be the only university giving social work training. In 2001 one year of English training was added to the curriculum making it a five years course. Since 1983 more than 3000 students have graduated as social workers from Hacettepe University but this number is insufficient to cover the growing needs of Turkey in this field. It is very important that more universities and schools are opened and the social services profession becomes more popular so that a sufficient number of graduates can fulfil the needs of the country.

In 2002 a private university the Baskent University in Ankara initiated a Department of Social work attached to the Health Sciences Department. This was the first step to realise this mission. This Department admits high school graduates for a five years course commencing with one year of English language. Baskent University, School of social work has applied for admission to the International Association of School of Social work (IASSW). Hacettepe University, School of Social work has been a member of (IASSW) since 1965.

GENERALISTIC APPROACH IN SOCIAL WORK

As social work has developed as a profession, there have been many new approaches to practice. In recent years the most familiar methods were case work, group work and community organisation. Practitioners were educated primarily in one skill area (e.g. children and families or policy and administration). A generalist practitioner needs competency in a wide variety of areas instead of being limited to a single track.

Generalist efforts are focused on understanding the individual and whole international system including its demands, supports and interrelationships. The generalist orientation allows the social worker to respond not only to an immediate problem of the individual, but also the conditions in the community and society that present barriers. The generalist social worker might work with the individual to meet individual needs and at the same time to work with agencies, organisations, institutions or the community to change conditions that created obstacles for that individual. It uses holistic assessment rather than driven by predetermined methods.

Generalist social work is one way of viewing practice that is a perspective focusing on the interface between systems with equal emphasis on the goals of social justice, humanising systems and improving the well being of people. The initial level of generalist practice consists of five elements:

- Multilevel problem-solving methodology;
- A multiple theoretical orientation including an ecological system model;
- A knowledge, value and skill base that is transferable;
- Selection of strategies or roles for intervention

According to Miley, O'Melia and DuBais, the generalist approach to social work practice rests on four major premises:

- First, human behaviour is connected to the social and physical environment.
- Second, based on this linkage among persons and environments, opportunities for enhancing the functioning of any human system includes changing the system itself, modifying its interactions with the environment and altering other systems within its environment. Generalist practitioners implement multilevel assessments and multi method interventions in response to these possible changes.
- Third, work with any level of human system-from individual to the society- uses similar social work processes.
- Finally, generalist practitioners have responsibilities also to work on social policies and to conduct and apply research.

For these reasons, in generalist approach all social workers need to develop essential social work skills and also interventive activity is based first on the needs of the client system. The social work process mentioned above is based largely on a scientific model and is strongly dependent on systems theory. There is a dynamic interplay of the phases of this process. Most theorists seem to agree that, the following phases are included in the process:

1. Initiating of the situation or problem,
2. Assessment of the situation or problem,
3. Goal setting and determination of task,
4. Action phase-task performed according to planned change strategies,
5. Termination,
6. Evaluation of the phase changed effort.

Although the agency setting is important to determine boundaries of work, the generalist worker must process skills effective in dealing with any size client system. He/she must be prepared to deal with private troubles as well as public issues. It is the aim of the generalist practitioner, from a holistic frame of reference, to deal with a client system in a manner most relevant to the client's needs and with the client's participation in the process.

Generalist Approach

Social work education from 1961-1995 continued using the traditional methodology approach. But during this time three syllabus changes were made but still retaining the same approach. Changes were made where necessary according to the needs of the community, new courses were incorporated and numbers of organisations where practical work could be conducted were increased. After 1980 social work educating groups following international scientific publications noticed a change in ideas and a more generalist outlook in social work care in North America and in Europe and they were influenced by this approach.

On the other hand in Turkey it was noticed in times that structure of the social services was not in accord with the education given and students who took case work, group work and community organisation separately had difficulties when practising. Because in many cases needs of the clients, which could be an individual, or a group of people or a society, cannot be solved by applying one single method therefore the social workers are the professionals who must work in every field and must be able to put their professional skill and gains into practice. In Turkey Structure of the social work organisations shows that there is no need for the social work profession to be specialised.

It is an undisputed reality that the duties of the social workers in the society determine the coverage of social work education. With this reality at hand a study has been initiated to determine a new suitable education approach to meet the needs of the society. With this purpose a survey was conducted in 1999 to learn the views of the social workers in Turkey on the social work education. A questionnaire was posted to 276 social workers in 38 provinces only 97 were returned answered. But the reason for this was probably that the disastrous earthquake that year meant those social workers were continuously working in turn in the earthquake stricken areas.

The results of the questionnaire showed that social work methods were not effectively used in the field. The most frequently used method of work was casework (76.3%). The least used method of work was group work (58.8%). A large proportion of social workers stated that they found it difficult to decide which method to use for each client or group. Other problems noted were lack of supervision or support from more experienced colleagues and the profession's not has been widely known by the public.

The social workers that answered the questionnaire also made various suggestions on the style and content to improve the social service education. Actually "inconsistent educational experience for students preparing to enter the social work profession and confusion on the part of employing agencies regarding the competencies they can expect from the graduates of these programmes are two important subjects for the social workers. If social work education programmes are to provide appropriate curricula to prepare graduates for such practice it is essential that professional community generate relevant debate on this matter and arrive at some common understanding".

It must be well understood and be kept in mind that changes to be made in the social work education will affect the social status of the social workers, their roles and functions. So the social work students in Turkey must receive education suitable to their field of work. To realise this following decisions have been taken on the subject:

— Method based education to be discontinued,

— Problem based education to be extended,

— The curricula should be reorganised according to generalist principles.

Looking at the problem from all sides makes it necessary that social work methods must be functionally used with the structural holistic approach and much closer interdisciplinary relations to be developed. Problem based educational approach makes the students to understand the problem in the international and national scales and makes them to have an idea how these problems will have effects on the individuals, on the families and on the small groups. There is a growing recognition that social workers should be prepared with a broad practice approach. This type of practice starts with assessing client needs and then selecting from a wide repertoire of intervention methods and theoretical perspectives that respond to those needs.

In the generalist approach after having put all the methods together professional knowledge and practice take shape according to the general frame. Generalist approach looks at human and society problems holistically and systematically and in practice it focuses on to the problem areas. With this it has an interdisciplinary character. In the direct and indirect social work applications in Turkey social workers in any case are not working with the "method based approach" but with the "problem based approach". After having recognised the problem they plan and execute micro, mezzo and macro interventions to eliminate the problem. Because of this by giving education in accord with the practice will improve theory-practice wholeness.

Structure of Social Work Education

Social work education in both schools in Turkey is given with the generalist approach. The education after high school, including one year of English is five years. There hasn't been any student yet who has not graduated with this generalist approach. Because of this at present its success in the field is not known. As future's social worker candidates, personalities of the students are very important.

Students are admitted to the school according to the result of the examination held by the "Higher Education Council". Admitting students with the pre interview system, which was used in the past is not being used now. On the other hand because of some problems involved relating to the examination system, students cannot choose their subject of education quite knowingly. There is an increasing possibility that students come to study social work quite by chance. Students finish high school at the age of 18. If a student doesn't fail he would finish the social work education at the age of 23. It is quite debatable that if these graduates at the age of 23 have or haven't acquired the maturity which a social worker is expected to have. Because, social work profession needs social and psychological mature personality.

The courses, which form the basis of social work, determined by Schotz, Jenkins and Sheafer are also given in the social work schools in this country. These are, liberal arts base; social work knowledge base (biological, socio cultural, psychological, human development, systems and ecological perspective and social work/social welfare history); Social work purpose, focus on person in environment; professionalism; sanction to practice, social work values and philosophy; basic communication skills; Ethnic/diversity, sensitivity; change process directed at problem resolution; understanding human relationships.

The overall purpose of the schools of social work in Turkey is to prepare students for the professional practice of social work at basic and advanced levels. The educational objectives of the undergraduate course are to enable students to integrate the knowledge, values and skills of the social work profession into competent practice with the client system of various sizes (micro, mezzo, macro) and types in the urban and rural areas; to prepare professional social workers for increased competence in their field of practice or leadership roles in administration, social planning, teaching, consultation, supervision and social research; to prepare graduates who are aware of their responsibility to continue their professional growth and development.

Undergraduate curriculum also includes social and economic justice, social welfare policy and services, social work theory and practice, research, field practicum and project seminars. Education includes extensive classroom activity as well as direct supervised work with clients-field placement. A variety of teaching and assessment methods are used within the programme. Emphasis is given to student participation.

The social workers that graduate from the schools of social work have many varied opportunities in both the public and private sectors. They work at Prime Ministry, Ministry of Health, Ministry of Education, Ministry of Justice, The Social Services and Child Protection Agency, Universities, Ministry of Labour and Social Security, Local Administration and its related Units, Crises Centres, Non Governmental Organisations and Foundations and in the Private Sector.

A training Ground for Social work Students

The type and quality of field experience in social work and other disciplines is an important area of study, relative to skill competencies, and the impacts on participants. This is not to say that it should not be challenging and demanding, rather the first year generalist field instructional experience should provide a healthy start and broad community spectrum to a social work career.

The more specialised second year field instructional experience should build on and enhance the generalist skills and academic knowledge gained in course work and the first year field practice. Kissman and Tran highlighted the importance of quality field training, where they postulated that the importance of field placements in social work education could hardly be overemphasised. Since social work is an "applied discipline, much emphasis is placed on socialising students into the profession by providing hands-on experience in the field".

Tolson and Kopp indicated that many traditional placements are in an agency setting with some combination of experiential and academic components, where "the level of learning has not been evaluated consistently... the most important influence on social work practice is the practicum". Rodgers and Williams suggested that because a social work student may spend half of their educational experience in a practice setting, field instruction should be considered a most valuable aspect of the training process. It is therefore important to include multiple options for field experience along with coursework offerings that enhance the particular type of placement. This concept applies well to the next area of discussion, which will focus on field placements and community practice.

Field Instruction

The importance of teaching group as well as community practice skills and theory in social work and related disciplines cannot be stated strongly enough. Brzuzy and Segal suggested that "teaching students to understand, appreciate, and use research based in the community" is desperately needed in social work education. Many schools of social work have no community development courses available and group courses are limited, many times to one advanced course in group theory.

The tasks that most social workers perform in their daily jobs are entrenched in community ideology. In order to perform these tasks adequately some expertise in community practice is necessary. For example, Birnbam and Auerbach found "graduate social work education has practically eliminated group work as a specialised area of study, and students in foundation courses learn little about group work theory and have limited or no group field work experience in which to develop practice skills".

According to Kurland and Salmon,, "requirements for concentrations offer a unique opportunity to add depth and sophistication to the teaching of group work and to better prepare students for the demands of contemporary professional practice, which requires a great amount of substantive expertise". This expertise can be applied to micro, mezzo, and macro practice in the larger community as well as the agency setting.

The current paradigms evolving from CSWE seem to be changing direction toward more generalist foci in social work education, which is supportive of the broader scope that group and community practices offer. Elliott indicated that social work interventions are predominantly delivered through a residual service delivery model. Elliot indicated that in social work today, a large degree of privatisation and the logical positivist research model is prevalent alongside a medical model of intervention, both of which address individual pathology. "This combination does not fully represent the social work tradition that along with individual change has always aimed to also encompass social action, social change, and community development".

Training students in the theory and methodology of community practice through placements in the community and focused directly on the community is one way of accomplishing this goal, which is also a timely focus for social work researchers. Coulton stated that "compared to our knowledge of individuals and families, research attention to the functioning of communities has been scant".

Because social work has a long-standing relationship with varied community based practices, sociological theories, and principles of group dynamics as they apply to individual functioning in the context of community, the opportunities for research through studying social work students in community placements are vast.

There is little doubt that with the current globalised economic conditions and changing roles for social workers, alternative training options need to be considered; where changes from for profit, nonprofit, and governmental agencies are resulting in social crises at all levels of service provision. Providing services in the community, in the home, etc. may become more the norm than the exception.

The nonprofit and government sectors, in which most social workers practice, will face great challenges in dealing with local social problems and needs. Social work practitioners, managers, students, and faculty must be prepared to recognise and seize the opportunities in these crises and to use knowledge, research, and practice skills to develop and strengthen community-based practice and service models. They will also need to build policy and research agendas that are grounded in community and family development.

The way to achieve this is through field training experiences, grounded in community practices, coordinated by well-established community curricula for the classroom experience, and includes greater balance between prevention, development, and remediation. Universities need to consider being "partners in promoting" community involvement and interdisciplinary social work. True generalist practitioners need to possess a holistic approach that emphasises the environment as well as the person. There is a need for an expanded community-oriented focus in social work education and field instruction.

To achieve connections between social work education, the practice community, and the larger cultural community students could be placed in a neighbourhood network rather than in a single agency, where they can experience the "context" of services as well as perform a variety of social work roles. Such placements might offer enough variety to be used for more than one year. This practice in "neighbourhoods and communities" needs to be based on solid social work perspectives with focus on "changing the culture of what is seen as valued, possible, and appropriate in these communities, which in turn will modify the opportunity systems for children and families".

Community oriented field placements

Models and techniques for community practice have been with us for some time and social work history is rich with community oriented practices, and providing alternative field placement opportunities along with the more traditional individual agency-based field placements, is a responsible way to reflect this domain of practice. Community development programmes are on the cutting edge of social work practice, and it is encouraging to see innovative schools of social work developing field-training experiences that include alternative models.

The community oriented model that is the focus of the following study exposes students to a wide array of challenges that result in them being better prepared as social work practitioners, policy makers, administrators, educators and researches, within the spectrum of community practice.

Winslow project

The project took place in the small Northern Arizona desert community of Winslow, with a 12,325 population, located on historic U. S. Route 66. This multi-phase project provided a cross-cultural and interstate generalist community development practicum, for Ohio State University social work master's students.

It was conducted on-site and was funded through a partnership between business constituencies with interests in Winslow, civic and community organisations on-site, private donors, and the students involved in the project. The student interns were able to pursue increasing levels of involvement in overlapping spheres of intervention. These spheres include:

- Creation and maintenance of a civic association, community micro-enterprise confederation in the underdeveloped, principally Hispanic neighbourhoods of Coopertown and Southside, which included community-based, needs assessment longitudinal research.
- Development and provision of ongoing violence prevention and citizenship enhancement programmes for elementary and high school students.
- Coordination and improvement of citywide social service, church, civic, and business collaborative networking to create a national model for community-building for the 21st century, and
- Traditional placements in various social service agencies in and around Winslow, with emphasis on networking, and collaborative interrelated wrap-around service provision.

The Centre for Peace Studies and Community Development in Columbus, Ohio administered this project in conjunction with its role as a Field Internship Agency for Ohio State's College of Social Work and relative to its various community development activities. The executive director for The Centre for Peace Studies and Community Development, William D. Eldridge, Ph.D., was the project director and is a full time faculty member in the College of social work.

Conjoint on site weekly classes in community development were required of all student participants as they are a requirement for all field placements. Residence and activity offices were located at Madre de Dios Catholic Church in Coopertown, a sub community in

Winslow. All operations for the Winslow project began at the Madre de Dios church and many of the community functions took place there as well.

The field placement involved students completing their first year (MSW I) generalist field experience as required by The Ohio State University Masters of Social Work programme. This first year fieldwork design was a block placement, conducted between June and August of the summer following the students' first year of academic course work. The Winslow project integrated student cohort team building, Hispanic American and Native American cultural learning, personal experience, and comprehensive community services into a consolidated eight-week period.

The students assumed their professional roles approximately six days per week, ten hours per day, through the eight-week project. This constitutes a total community service commitment of approximately 480 contact service hours. The students actually exceeded the typical non-block first year placement of 320 hours. The extra hours was considered volunteer time, which the students had contractually agreed to when, accepting the field placement.

Sample

Twenty-one students took part in the Winslow Project. Of the seven students who participated during the summer of 1997, there were six females and one male. The mean age for the females was 27.8 years, while the male students' age was 57 years. All of the students had social work employment history and three were volunteers who had already completed their field placements before this project. Among the 14 students participating during the second summer of 1998, there were 12 females and 2 males.

The mean age for the females was 27.4 with the youngest being 20 years and the oldest 34. The mean age for the males was 23.5 aged 23 and 24 respectively. One of the female students was an upper level social work undergraduate and not in an official field placement. The students that participated in this experience assumed a good deal of the cost including their airfare and some food costs. The Winslow experience involved these students living together as a group in dormitory housing.

Project activities

The students were involved in a variety of different, but related, service delivery functions. Personal learning consultations, team evaluation, and cohort feedback procedures were parts of their generalised first year learning experience. The students also met together for training throughout the nine months before their experience in Winslow; which focused on preparing them to work and relate effectively and compassionately within the cultures and environment they discovered in Arizona. During these training sessions, they also worked on group cohesiveness, which would prove beneficial to them later.

While in Winslow, they were engaged in learning about community-based practice while actually residing together as a small group microcosm, while at the same time spending eight weeks working with community leaders, adults, families, and children in and around Winslow. The needs of the community and the agency involvement added to the experiential foundation of the Winslow project.

The project also involved specific task objectives as follows

— Develop and support a neighbourhood residents (civic) association.

- Develop a leadership coalition in the Hispanic neighbourhoods of Coopertown and Southside.
- Work with children on literacy and anti-violence programmes.
- Assist in various social service activities on the Hopi and Navajo Reservations.
- Assist adults and teenagers with career planning activities.
- Conduct individual and family counselling sessions.
- Facilitate small group meetings related to community projects.
- Network and conduct community cooperation planning functions among human service organisations.
- Create plans and needs assessments for micro-enterprise development, and provide physical labour to help build parks, repair homes, etc.

Each student worked and learned as a member of smaller teams with other students, community members, and professionals; and had an opportunity to be involved in a range of differing activities from which their experiences and newly acquired skills and knowledge were shared with other teams and within the whole student community.

As described, the students all resided, ate, slept, and worked together. They slept in bunk beds with three to four persons per bedroom. In this context, one of the most significant aspects of this internship was the opportunity for them to become a community in the process of learning and caring for each other, while also engaging the exterior community neighbourhoods. The project provided the opportunity for these two communities to develop simultaneously.

Winslow provided a rich and extraordinary opportunity to learn about and work with members of the Southwestern Hispanic community. The social work students were able to work extensively with the Hopi and Navajo Native American Tribes living in Winslow, and on adjacent reservations just north of the city. The students attended cultural orientation lectures and group training seminars.

The focus of these workshops was to formally learn about Hispanic, Native American, and Southwestern cultures. Their experiences provided many learning opportunities. Some of the learning challenges included solving conflicts within their own group and with one another, living in a new environment, being away from family and friendship supports in Ohio, and "becoming a group." These contexts of the experience created a symbiotic developmental process as the students, the community members and, the two communities conjoined and separated many times during the processes of community development.

Research questions

The writer and the project director developed research questions focused on the experiences and knowledge gained by internship participants, as follows:

— Are there changes in feelings/attitudes related to community practice for the students that chose to take part in this field placement experience?

— Is there any perceived personal or professional growth for these students through this experience?

— What is the Programme Director's evaluation of the student's progress and the project?

The study included a longitudinal/multi-baseline, ABA (pre-test-interim-posttest) research design, focusing on the students and their perceived and observed experiential growth and learning processes, as well as the perceptions of the programme director related to these dynamics. These variables were extracted and analysed through narrative analysis of written self-report and observation during the experience.

Data collection

Data collection included:

1. an initial questionnaire session one month prior to each group of students leaving for Winslow,
2. an on-site mid-term questionnaire and observation session at week five in Winslow and,
3. a follow-up questionnaire session one month following each group's return from Winslow.

The same interviewer administered the questionnaire at the three data collection sessions by the. The mid-term and follow-up sessions included the original interview questions slightly altered to elicit information about how students had applied their learning to their present situations. The questions contained a significant focus on community, community-based practice, and identity as social workers, social work field experience, and the student's feelings about these topics.

The researcher acquired the observation data through the two-on-site visits and the follow-up interview with the project director. The data is narrative in nature and therefore, evaluated through this analysis method. The outcome variables relate to the concept that students can benefit from an experience like the Winslow Project.

Questionnaire data

The questionnaire contained multi-layered items focusing on community, community-based practice, field experience, and the students' feelings about the experience. The questionnaire also assessed student's goals of the project and relationship dynamics within the student groups, beginning with questions regarding the student's expectations of the experience, to elicit their projections of what the Winslow experience could provide related to their field instruction, personal, and professional growth. The follow-up questionnaire included questions that asked if the experience had met expectations.

As evidenced by the data, all 21 students believed that they were meeting their expectations at mid-point and 19 reported that they had met or exceeded their expectations at follow-up. Among the expectations reported as met by the students, are the following. Twelve students reported better communication skills, ten improved assertiveness skills, twenty increased cultural awareness, twenty-one achieved better relationship skills, nineteen gained in social work practice skills, twenty-one added community development experience, fifteen increased their sense of self-awareness, seventeen reported gains in spiritual growth, fifteen felt they grew emotionally, and ten described better general well being.

An interesting phenomenon observed during this experience was that the students began to see their group as a community early on, with 19 out of the 21 students describing their group as a community with all of the characteristics and roles that would be expected. It was during this process that the concept of the student group as a community began to develop and expand.

The cohesiveness of the group was also significant in this data set in that, all of the students reported that they felt bonded with their fellow group members at mid-point. The purpose of question one was to elicit this information. The purpose of question 2 was to elicit each student's concept of community and then to apply that concept to the student group, to measure growth relative to knowledge of community. The initial definitions related to what constitutes a community were consistent as applied to groups of people in similar situations.

All 21 students agreed that community involves some form of mutual focus and working together. Twenty reported their student groups were able to meet this criterion and thus develop as communities while working in the larger community of Winslow. The students described their groups as typical communities, with the relationships and conflicts consistent with the dynamics of community. There was a definite change in the way the students viewed community throughout the experience as evidenced by 19 students remaining consistent with their responses throughout the process.

These students first described community as groups of people who all have one characteristic in common, live in a shared area, have shared interests, etc. At mid-point 16 students expanded the definition to groups of people whom live near one another and interconnect in their development and prosperity. Finally, at follow-up, 18 students described community as independent personalities that work together for a common cause, have shared strengths and goals, are mutually committed to the whole, etc. When asked to apply these concepts to the groups, the students again showed their cohesion and community growth.

The members of the cohorts spoke fondly of one another and related that the group members became very close, although there was some resentment stated by six students related to a few members who did not perform as expected by the majority, though there was much resistance by these students to label them. When asked to talk about the problems in the group, these six students responses included the following:

— The group works well together overall.

— It was nice to have such a group of people with such diverse personalities and styles.

— The group got along better than expected.

For the most part, we worked well together although at time there was a bit of strain due to so many independent personalities. It is interesting that one can view the process for these students in terms of their changing perspective of community. The idea of bonding with others in a way that connects the larger whole or that community has a dynamic of family or people who are connected suggests the cohesiveness of the students as groups. Question 3 follows the same concepts as question number two. The difference here is that the students were to define community development related to social work practice.

The hypothesis here is that the Winslow experience will enhance the definition of social work practice and community development for these students. The purpose of question one was to elicit this information. The simple definition at the beginning changed at mid-point and follow-up. The cohorts started with a standard textbook definition of social work in the community, moved to an appreciation of community building as a long-term process, and finally to working at community building from within the community.

The students redefined their concept of social work in the community throughout the experience, constituting a transition from individual change agent to active participant in a larger collaborative, contextual, and interdependent process. The students appear to have realised the complexity of communities. Their willingness to allow for and respect differences increased through trial and error during this experience. Their realisation was that social workers do not bring people together for community practice as much as they "practice life" with and among people through active problem solving and planning.

The data indicates that the students conceptualise community building as not something that you do to a community but rather, it is an experiential process that involves people and their collective evolvement. Each student shared their feelings about personal relationships and the importance of these in their lives. The focus was on family and friendships on the initial questionnaire, and on the group members and community on the mid-term and follow-up questionnaires.

The results showed growth in relation to group cohesiveness over the experience and, the level of commitment between group members to one another and to the group as a whole. It was interesting to see the struggle that these students took part in as they attempted to redefine their concept of community. The idea of their group as a community or family was foreign to their prior beliefs about what community was. By the end of this experience, the students reported achievement and growth as the result of the relationships formed and, that constant contact with others was an essential element to the group development.

The concept of family, advocacy, social action and interdependency all became themes for these students, and concepts of location, common goals, group as a community, and the ability to be tolerant of others were reported as positive outcomes of this experience. In the next data set, the object was to elicit students' feelings and thoughts about how they performed in their field placement and in their student community. It sought to get the students to self-assess their roles in these teams, as well as, the larger community of Winslow.

One student described the role of caretaker in the beginning, which seemed to continue as time progressed.

Another described roles in terms of task orientation, which remained consistent throughout the experience, which is an outcome that might be expected. Another group of students were able to define their task roles well initially, but by the end of the process, they described a combination of task and group roles.

From family roles to group roles was the transition for these students. Some stated the roles were not clear and indicated that they would have preferred more structure, while others thrived on the challenges of the unknown. There were several self-proclaimed leaders in the groups and though these are characteristics most often described by the other students as problematic, they can be very positive in the practice of community development.

The main result presented as a feeling of achievement and, even though the students may have seen their roles as static and not changing much, they related that the roles they assumed were more beneficial due to the experience. The goal of self-assessment continued as students began to look inward for the answers and discover what it was about them that enhanced this experience. The data showed evidence of a difference in thinking related to the concept of responsibility as applied to self, other individuals, and communities.

The process of learning as evidenced by self-report showed an eagerness to learn and grow as a student community. They recognised and confronted some of their own behaviours and applied the needed changes. The nature of the Winslow experience allowed for this self-evaluation to take place through the challenges faced outside the comfort zone of home, time spent in contemplation in the desert, and in personal meetings with Dr. Eldridge.

The reported values remained consistent throughout the experience and the student's were able to apply these to the experience without much conflict. There was reported insight into recognising their limitations and utilising the strengths of others as a way of maintaining balance. Other characteristics were the ability to be flexible and remain strength based, openness, seeing humour and caring about others, putting strengths into action, utilising self as a tool, and acceptance of the opinion of others.

When stated their goals and evaluated them, the data indicated patterned wishes to be more active and social, and less withdrawn, along with goals related to an inner sense of peace and self-nurturing. The opportunity to challenge self in such a way as to take some new risks, learning to live with and get along with the group, and interacting with people from Hispanic and Native American cultures were goals that were achieved. Some students had seen the initial goals as being different somehow then the outcomes, but the transition process suggests the outcomes and goals were not different at all.

The ability to learn about ones' self and apply this knowledge was a positive outcome of this field experience; and the experience provided a means for self-assessment and change and, in the process, challenged assumptions and concepts that interns brought into the experience. The work related to "just getting along" with others in the group environment was challenging in itself while the students reported that the greatest challenges were dealing with their own agendas.

The Winslow experience provided a catalyst for solidifying the blend of students and the cultures that they were involved in, and the process of identifying their roles and goals helped them identify insights gained and the changes made. The final question allowed students to add any final comments to the experience. Closure and the ability to gain a synopsis of the student's feelings was the desire. Some of the feelings shared focused on relationships among group members.

The most positive note was that the students were able to recognise their own potential and the importance of the learning experience as a whole. Many of them described the experience as rewarding, challenging, fulfilling and, had met their expectations. One student related satisfaction with the experience and rated it as the greatest of their life. They agreed that they were able to learn more about self in the process of dealing with others in the group, and these relationships were their greatest challenges at times.

There was an expressed need for more prior training, which might have enhanced the preparation for this experience, including prior coursework on the local culture and customs, theory and method of community development, and race and ethnicity coursework that includes more focus on Hispanic American and Native American information. The strength of the group experience and the process of applying personal growth and experiential learning to personal and professional settings were follow-up goals for some of the students. The students as a whole reported that their coursework in this area was limited to race with little focus on cultures.

Project directors

The Project Director, William D. Eldridge, Ph.D. was asked by the researcher to narratively address four content areas in a review of the two-year Winslow Project, including the impact on the community of Winslow and the future of social work in terms of such projects. The four content areas were knowledge of community, knowledge of community development, cohort development among the students, and community outcomes.

The response to this topic area indicated there is no better way to "learn very quickly about a community other than actually living in the community." This data suggests that the knowledge of community continues far beyond the Winslow experience and many of the students supported this in their responses to the questionnaires. One point made in the interview was that if the project continued it would include "story telling" about the community as an introduction to Winslow.

This situation would include ten or fifteen people invited to come together and tell the Winslow story; the students and possibly other people in the community could be the audience. As they relate their story through pictures, videos, audiotapes, narrative, or anecdotal discussions the knowledge of community enhances. Knowledge about community and community involvement are synonymous terms when viewed from a pragmatic perspective, as are social work and community ideologies.

Another salient point is the need for concentrations in community development at schools of social work. Because the students "really don't have any knowledge of community development," it was necessary to teach a concurrent course while they were on-site, although they need far better preparation in terms of the theory and methodology of community practice. The ideal would be to move community development and community theory academic courses to the first-year and then have second year students involved in Winslow type field placements.

There is agreement that if this would most likely contradict CSWE requirements that the first year placement be generic, while the second year placement is specific. However, it was concluded, "a community development placement is very clearly an example of generalist practice." The ideal would be to have generalist practice orientation be part of the second year scenario, which provides students the opportunity to complete courses in community development and community practice in the first year.

Finally, "the greatest advantage of community practice outcomes is start up activities, followed in subsequent years by more comprehensive work putting icing on the various components of the cake that are built in previous sessions." It is important to finish what we start and this requires follow-up. The follow-up could utilise telephone interviews, e-mail, the Internet, or other means of contact. Follow-up community evaluation, "particularly when you have a neighbourhood association that is built comes through a local indigenous organisation that remains after the students depart." The continuation of the projects and activities initiated by the students while in Winslow are evidence of positive outcomes as well.

Promoting community-based experiences in social work education is important and exemplified within the primary service interventions for the Winslow project. All the information presented points to the fact that these students benefited from the Winslow experience in many ways. Learning to work as team members and challenging themselves in a new environment was an important element of their learning. This study investigated the concepts of community, community development, and social work in communities.

In the processes of analysing the experiences of the twenty-one students, the research questions acted as filters for the information. The following includes a summary of each research question and student responses.

First, are there any differences in feelings/attitudes for the students taking part in this field placement experience? The narrative responses of the students support this outcome and suggest that students gained knowledge during their experience.

Secondly, many reported that they would practice social work differently because of the impact of this experience, and many reported they would repeat this experience again if given the chance. This is a testimonial to this experience repeated many times during the interview process with both cohorts.

Third, what is the Programme Director's evaluation of the student's progress and the project? As was presented in the Programme Director's narrative there are many benefits to this type of placement, including service delivery to communities along with personal & cohort development among interns. The need for more support and community focus at schools of social work was also postulated. The impact of this type of training is supported in the data presented.

Implications

Review of study

Because the profession of social work has a longstanding relationship with community-based practices, community development and strengthening the bonds that support families and communities; students of social work could benefit from training within the community-based environment, as with the training received in the Winslow Project.

Attitudes and feelings

The narrative analysis of the questionnaire data sustained the reported differences in student feelings about themselves, the members of their group, and about the people and community of Winslow, where students believed that they were not only meeting their initial expectations but also exceeding them by the end of their experience.

Both groups of students indicated better communication skills, assertiveness skills, cultural awareness, relationship skills, social work practice skills, community development experience, self-awareness, spiritual growth, emotional growth, and general well being. As these are all related to self-growth, awareness, and social functioning they fit very nicely with the research question related to personal and professional growth.

Social work knowledge

Students saw their group as a community early on and presented this with all of the characteristics and roles that one might expect in a community. It was during this process that the concept of the student groups as a community began to develop and expand for both cohorts, suggesting the validity of the common Winslow internship experience.

The student's concepts of community expanded, and developed through the Winslow experience, including, growing cohesiveness of the groups, and struggles with their concepts of what community should be. They reported achievement and growth as the result of the relationships they formed, whereby constant contact with their group members was an essential element to the community identity and each person's identity as a member of that community.

The concept of family, advocacy, social action, interdependency, location, common goals, the group as a community, and the ability to be tolerant of others were positive outcomes of this experience. Their insight into the dynamics of community practice increased through the various experiences that were taking place. The concept of measuring how students feel about their field placements is not new. The importance here is that as these students were involved in many field placements in and around the Winslow community, though they were all related to one actual community placement.

In reviewing the data it appears that the ability to learn about ones' self and apply this knowledge is a positive outcome of the Winslow experience. The students suggested they "had been forever changed" through this experience and, that they would practice social work differently as a result.

The students in both cohorts suggested that this experience provided a means for self-assessment and change and, their involvement was rewarding, challenging, and fulfilling and as having met and exceeded their expectations. The community development course that was part of their field instruction was highly rated, though all agreed that coursework integrated into their first year curriculum would have enhanced this curriculum.

The final area for review here is the project directors' thoughts related to the experience of the students. It is important to note that this data closely mirrors the reported experiences of the students. The "group-block" field placement experience is a positive experiential method for training future community-oriented social work practitioners, and the profession of social work must be responsible for encouraging this opportunity. It was postulated that because social work includes theoretical frameworks from various disciplines and paradigms including but not limited to, sociology, psychology, anthropology, and political science that this phenomenon helps define social work as a profession.

Bibliography

Adler, P., & Adler, P., "Do university lawyers and the police define research values?", In W. C. Van Den Hoonard (Ed.), *Walking the tightrope: Ethical issues forqualitative researchers* (pp. 34-42), Toronto: University of Toronto Press, 2002.

Alvino, L. A., "Who's watching the watchdogs? Responding to the erosion of research ethics by enforcing promises", *Columbia Law Review*, 103, 893-924, 2003.

Burton, C., "Street says blight bill will lead to "world class neighborhoods", in: *Philadelphia Inquirer*, March 14, p.A1, 2002.

Caldeira, T., "Fortified enclaves: The new urban segregation", in: Holston, J. (ed.): Cities and citizenship, Durham: Duke University Press, pp. 114-138, 1999.

Davis, M., *City of quartz: Excavating the future in Los Angeles*, London: Verso, 1990.

Dear, M., *The postmodern urban condition*, California: Blackwell, 2000.

Fairbanks, R.P. II., *Retheorizing blight in Philadelphia: An analysis of the contemporary present*, Unpublished manuscript, University of Pennsylvania, 2002.

Fairbanks, R.P., II, *A theoretical primer on space, in: Critical Social Work*, 3, pp. 131-154, 2003.

Frumkin, M. and Lloyd, G. A., "Social Work Education", in: Edwards, R. L. and Hoppes, J. G. (eds.): *Encyclopaedia of Social Work*, 19th. Edition. Washington, D.C: NASW Press, 2001.

Patton, M., *Qualitative research and evaluation methods*, (3rd ed.), Thousand Oaks, CA: Sage, 2002.

Rubin, H., & Rubin, I., *Qualitative interviewing: The art of hearing data,* Thousand Oaks, CA.: Sage, 1995.

Stacey, J., "Can there be a feminist ethnography?" In S. Gluck & D. Patai (Eds.),*Women's words: The feminist practice of oral history* (pp. 111-119), New York:Routledge, 1991.

Temkin, K., & Rohe, W. M., *Social capital and neighborhood stability: An empirical investigation,* Housing Policy Debate, 9(1), 61-88, 1998.

Weil, M., *Community practice: Conceptual models,* Binghamton: Haworth Press, 1996.

Weiss, C. H., "Nothing as practical as a good theory: Exploring theory-based evaluation for comprehensive community initiatives for children and families", In J. P. Connell, A. C. Kubisch, L. B. Schorr, & C. H. Weiss (Eds.), *NewApproaches to Evaluating Community Initiatives,* 65-92, Washington, D.C.: The Aspen Institute, 1995.

Index